KNOWING THE SPIRIT

Colin Dye

Sovereign World

Sovereign World Ltd
PO Box 777
Tonbridge
Kent TN11 0ZS
England

Scriptural quotations are from the New King James Version, Thomas Nelson Inc., 1991.

ISBN 1 85240 201 6

Typeset by CRB Associates, Reepham, Norfolk
Printed in England by Clays Ltd, St Ives plc.

FOREWORD

The material in this *Sword of the Spirit* series has been developed over the past ten years at Kensington Temple in London as we have sought to train leaders for the hundreds of churches and groups we have established. Much of the material was initially prepared for the students who attend the International Bible Institute of London – which is based at our church.

Over the years, other churches and colleges have asked if they may use some of our material to help them establish training courses for leaders in their towns and countries. This series has been put together partly to meet this growing need, as churches everywhere seek to train large numbers of new leaders to serve the growth that God is giving.

The material has been constantly refined – by myself, by the students as they have responded, by my many associate pastors, and by the staff at the Bible Institute. In particular, my colleague Timothy Pain has been responsible for sharpening, developing and shaping my different courses and notes into this coherent series.

I hope that many people will use this series in association with our developing Satellite Bible School, but I also pray that churches around the world will use the books to train leaders.

We live at a time when increasing numbers of new churches are being started, and I am sure that we will see even more startling growth in the next few decades. It is vital that we re-examine the way we train and release leaders so that these new churches have the best possible biblical foundation. This series is our contribution to equipping tomorrow's leaders with the eternal truths that they need.

Colin Dye

CONTENTS

INTRODUCTION

Many ordinary people are puzzled by the idea of a Holy Spirit. They believe that Jesus lived on earth two thousand years ago. They feel that some sort of all-powerful being must exist 'somewhere out there'. But they struggle with the concept of a Spirit who is God and Jesus and himself, and who is both out there and right here.

Despite all the teaching about the Spirit in recent years, I suspect that there are still many believers who are puzzled by the Spirit. They know that they should consider him a person, but they cannot help thinking of him as an 'it', as an impersonal force like electricity. They believe they can be affected by him, but they do not think that they can know him in a wonderful personal way. They are not convinced that the Spirit is as distinctive and as real a person as Jesus.

There is a tremendous amount of talk about being 'led by the Spirit', 'filled with the Spirit', 'anointed with the Spirit', 'empowered by the Spirit', and so on. Yet most of this talk is focused on 'us'. *We* want to know what it will mean for *us* to be filled and empowered. We rarely concentrate on knowing *him* who desires to lead and fill us, or on discovering the Spirit's holy purpose behind *his* activity.

Some Christians seem to think that the Spirit appeared at Pentecost. Yet we can only truly know the Spirit and understand his ministry when we appreciate *all* that the Bible teaches about him. The Old Testament introduction to the Spirit is a vital foundation for any accurate understanding about him. We will misunderstand his work today if we ignore what he did before Pentecost.

By the end of this book, you will see that the Spirit is totally centred on Jesus. He convicts unbelievers about Christ and urges them to receive and respond to the Son. He brings about the new birth, by which sinners trust Christ and are initiated and introduced into Christ's body. He goes on revealing Christ – and the truth about him – to, in and through Christian believers. He witnesses to the fact that we are forever Christ's by giving us a foretaste of heaven. He equips us to serve Christ, to serve with Christ, and to serve like Christ. And he transforms us into the likeness of Christ. He is all about Jesus Christ!

This book is essentially for those believers who will set aside their own ideas about the Holy Spirit and will study God's word to discover God's revelation about the Spirit. Please make sure that you read each scriptural reference – and tick the margin reference boxes as you go alone to show that you have. Please answer every question and think through each point as it is made. Before moving on to a new section, think carefully about the implications of what you have studied. Please allow God to speak to you as you study his word.

At the end of the book, there is some activity material. Make sure that you study Parts 1–9 before working through the activities, as this will ensure that you have an overview of the biblical teaching about the Spirit before you try to apply the details of one area. The activities will help you to grasp and to apply the material you have studied.

You will also be able to use the activity pages when you teach the material to small groups. Please feel free to photocopy these pages and distribute them to any group you are leading. Although you should work through all the activities when you are studying on your own, please don't expect a small group to cover all the activity material. Instead, prayerfully select those parts that you think are most relevant for your group. This means that, at some meetings you might use all the material whilst at others you might use only a small part.

By the time that you have finished working through this book, it is my prayer that you will know God's wonderful Holy Spirit more fully, that you will have entered into an even deeper relationship with him, and that you will have started to experience the joy of living in and with the glorious presence of Christ.

Colin Dye

PART ONE

the spirit in the old testament

Throughout the Old Testament, the Holy Spirit is called 'the Spirit' or 'the Spirit of God'. The English word 'Spirit' is always a translation of the Hebrew word *ruach*. It is vital we grasp what this word means.

THE BLOWING OF GOD

Like most of the biblical words which refer to God, *ruach* is a picture-word with a vivid and precise meaning. It always carries the idea of breath being blown out – as when we blow up a balloon, or blow out a candle, or pant heavily during a hard race.

The idea behind *ruach* is vigorously moving air – even violently moving air. *Ruach* suggests a release of energy, an invading force, the exercise of power, dynamic activity evidencing life.

In some places *ruach* describes a wind which is immensely powerful, even destructive. But it is always under God's control and it always effects his will. We can see this in Genesis 8:1; Exodus 10:13–19; 14:21; 15:10; Numbers 11:31; 1 Kings 19:11; Job 1:19; 37:21; Psalm 1:4; 48:7; 107:25; 135:7; 147:18; 148:8; Isaiah 7:2; 12:15; 27:8; 41:16; Jeremiah 10:13; 49:36; 51:1; Ezekiel 5:2–12; 13:11–13; 27:26; 37:9; Daniel 7:2; Hosea 13:15; Jonah 1:4; 4:8 and Zechariah 2:6.

These *ruach* passages suggest that the Spirit of God is a hurricane whom we cannot control or predict. He is an invading force who transforms wherever he blows. He is God's power in action.

These verses show that Spirit is the wind who comes straight from God's mouth. This is why some people have called him 'the breath of God'. It is his activity which proves that God is alive. But – even more than that – he is also the breath without which all men and women are dead.

Ruach literally means breathing out with great violence. This is not a picture of a gentle breeze. Instead, it is a picture of God taking a deep breath and blowing as hard as he can! In Ezekiel 37:1–14 the Spirit, God's breath, brings dead bones to life and moulds them into a powerful army.

In Ezekiel 37:1–14, the one Hebrew word *ruach* is translated in quick succession as 'breath', 'wind' and 'Spirit'. This shows that the picture-word *ruach* has a wide range of associations. It is used in the scriptures to show:

- God's Spirit – personal, purposeful, invisible and irresistible

- individual human consciousness – as in the word 'soul'

- the wind which rustles leaves and flattens buildings

There is no English word which carries all of these associations. The English word 'blow' can mean the breathing out of air by a human and the force of the wind, but 'blow' does not refer to the intellectual, spiritual and emotional individuality of God and human beings.

On the other hand, the English word 'Spirit' does denote conscious personhood, but it does not carry any commonly understood association of violent wind and breath.

This means that we must take great care when we are reading about God's Spirit in the Old Testament. He is God's *ruach* – God's 'blowing' – and this *always* suggests God's power in action.

WORD PICTURES

The Spirit is described in the Old Testament in four more images which help us grasp his character and appreciate his activities more fully.

1.   Water

The Bible uses water as a symbol of God's blessing and spiritual refreshment in passages like Psalm 36:9; 46:4; Isaiah 30:25; 55:1; Jeremiah 2:13; 17:13; Joel 3:18; Zechariah 13:1 and 14:8.

In Ezekiel 47:1–12, the prophet saw water flowing out from the heart of God's future temple. This pure water represented the unrestricted flow of God's blessings to his people, and Ezekiel was ordered to go on immersing himself deeper and deeper in the water!

Jeremiah 2:13 & 17:13 describe God as a 'fountain of living waters', and John 7:37–39 tells us that this is a picture of the Holy Spirit.

There are two obvious uses of water:

- it is essential to life

- it is vital for washing

In Old Testament times, armies tried to cut off the water supply when they attacked an enemy as they knew that all people die quickly without water.

Water is also used for cleaning. It was used in Exodus 29:4 & Numbers 8:7 to consecrate Priests and Levites for service; in Leviticus 11:40; 15:5–33 to remove defilement from people; and in Ezekiel 36: 25–28 God promised to clean us with water and make us new people.

These verses help build a picture of the Spirit's activity. He is God's blessing, and we need him – God's water – for life and cleansing.

2.   Fire

Fire is even more effective than water at purifying and refining. In the Old Testament, fire was a symbol of God's intervention in history and of the way his Spirit purified human hearts and cleansed them for service. This is seen most dramatically in Isaiah 6:6–9.

Psalm 36:9 ☐
46:4 ☐

Isaiah 30:25 ☐
55:1 ☐

Jeremiah 2:13 ☐
17:13 ☐

Joel 3:18 ☐

Zechariah 13:1 ☐
14:8 ☐

Ezekiel 47:1–12 ☐

Jeremiah 2:13 ☐
17:13 ☐

John 7:37–39 ☐

Exodus 29:4 ☐

Numbers 8:7 ☐

Leviticus 11:40 ☐
15:5–33 ☐

Ezekiel 36: 25–28 ☐

Isaiah 6:6–9 ☐

Genesis 15:17 ☐

Exodus 3:2 ☐

    13:21 ☐

    19:18 ☐

Deuteronomy
    4:11–12 ☐

Daniel 3:25 ☐

Kings 6:17 ☐

Deuteronomy
    4:24 ☐

Psalm 66:12 ☐

Isaiah 43:2 ☐

    66:15 ☐

Ezekiel 22:18–22 ☐

Zechariah 13:9 ☐

Malachi 3:2–3 ☐

    4:1 ☐

Isaiah 4:2–6 ☐

1 Samuel 10:1–9 ☐

    16:13 ☐

Isaiah 61:1 ☐

Zechariah 4:1–14 ☐

Isaiah 61:1–3 ☐

At times, when God revealed himself to people, he was surrounded by fire. For example, Genesis 15:17; Exodus 3:2; 13:21; 19:18; Deuteronomy 4:11–12 and Daniel 3:25.

In 2 Kings 6:17; Deuteronomy 4:24; Psalm 66:12; Isaiah 43:2; 66:15; Ezekiel 22:18–22; Zechariah 13:9; Malachi 3:2–3 & 4:1, fire revealed God's presence, his holiness, his judgement and his anger against sin. He called those whom he wanted to cleanse to pass through the fire.

Isaiah 4:2–6 shows that 'the spirit of burning' is a vital part of God's purifying work. This suggests that we need to be cleansed by the Spirit's – by God's fire – if we are to be called holy.

3.   Oil

In Old Testament days, oil had three practical uses. It was used:

- in cooking – to prepare food

- in the dark – to provide light

- in medicine – to aid healing

Each of these uses has an obvious spiritual application in the Spirit. However, it was the ceremonial use of oil to anoint priests and kings for service which was used as a picture of God's Spirit.

Anointing with oil symbolised the equipping of a priest or king for service with the necessary resource of God's Spirit. We can read about this in 1 Samuel 10:1–9; 16:13; Isaiah 61:1 and Zechariah 4:1–14.

When oil was poured over priests and kings as a picture of the Spirit, it showed that the Spirit would feed, enlighten and heal through the anointed person. This can be seen most clearly in Isaiah 61:1–3.

4.   Dove

Many think today that doves merely portray gentleness. But they had a much wider meaning in the Old Testament. In those days, doves were used in three distinct ways:

- they were a source of food

- they were sacrificed to God by the poor

- they carried messages

The dove in Genesis 8:1–12 announced the new creation and a new existence in the promises of God. The dove is revealed as the King's bride in Song of Songs 2:14, 5:2 & 6:9. Leviticus 5:7–10 shows the dove as an acceptable sacrifice for poor people.

The Hebrew word for dove is *Yonah*. This means that the man we know as the prophet Jonah is better understood as Mr Dove. He was the messenger of God who was sent on a mission to speak to sinners, and who spent three days in a fish's belly before his resurrection.

This suggests that, when the Spirit came down like a dove at Jesus' baptism, much more than gentleness was implied. The dove:

- showed that Jesus was a messenger who would feed God's people

- revealed that the dawn of a new creation had arrived

- pointed to Jesus as a sacrifice for poor people's sins

- hinted at a death and resurrection as part of a mission to reach sinners

- showed by its descent that Jesus was anointed with a Spirit who was all these things and who would bring them about in Jesus' life

THE WORK OF THE SPIRIT

The phrase 'the Spirit' or 'the Spirit of God' appears nearly one hundred times in the Old Testament. Every time it is used, it describes God at work, God bringing change, God making a difference to his world and his people. The scriptural material seems to show that God's Spirit is involved in seven main areas of activity.

1. He shapes creation

Genesis 1:2; 2:7; Psalm 33:6; Job 26:13; 33:4 describe how the Spirit moulds creation into shape and animates created beings.

Genesis 1:2 records the Spirit hovering over the waters, like a bird of prey waiting for the right moment to dive into action. Genesis 2:7 states that God breathed life into the nostrils of the being he had just

Genesis 8:1–12 ☐

Song of Songs
2:14 ☐
5:2 ☐
6:9 ☐

Leviticus 5:7–10 ☐

Genesis 1:2 ☐
2:7 ☐

Psalm 33:6 ☐

Job 26:13 ☐
33:4 ☐

shaped from dust – and it became a living being. What the Father had created, the Spirit animated – when he heard God's word. The Spirit, the blowing of God, the breath of God, dived into action, released God's life-giving power and cold dust became breathing humanity.

2.   He controls history

Psalm 104:29–30; Isaiah 34:16 & 40:7 illustrate the way the Spirit sustains life and controls the course of nature and history.

3.   He reveals God's truth and will

The Scriptures teach a strong association between the Spirit and the revelation of God's truth and will to his messengers the prophets. This is the basis of prophecy.

Moses' wish in Numbers 11:29 is the first hint of a link between the Spirit and prophecy. Saul's experiences in 1 Samuel 10 and 19:18–24 show that the Spirit's descent led to spontaneous prophecy. Micah 3:8 suggests that the Spirit not only supplied the inspiration but also gave the courage to deliver the revelation. And Joel 2:28 makes it clear that the coming of the Spirit should result in prophecy.

In Ezekiel 37:1–2, the Spirit brings the prophet to the valley of dry bones and reveals God's truths through a vision.

Many other verses show the Spirit revealing God's truth by distilled insight or direct communication. For example: Numbers 24:2; 2 Samuel 23:2; 2 Chronicles 12:18; 15:1; Nehemiah 9:30; Job 32:8; Isaiah 61:1–4; Ezekiel 2:2; 11:24 & Zechariah 7:12.

4.   He teaches the way of faithfulness

In Nehemiah 9:20; Psalms 143:10; Isaiah 48:16 & 63:10–14, the Spirit teaches God's truth – through prophetic revelations – to all God's people. He points out the ways of faithfulness and fruitfulness.

5.   He awakens people to God

We read about the Spirit waking men and women to the reality of God throughout the Old Testament. He convicts people about their sin.

Sidebar references:

Psalm 104:29–30 ☐

Isaiah 34:16 ☐
      40:7 ☐

Numbers 11:29 ☐

1 Samuel 10 ☐
      19:18–24 ☐

Micah 3:8 ☐

Joel 2:28 ☐

Ezekiel 37:1–2 ☐

Numbers 24:2 ☐

2 Samuel 23:2 ☐

2 Chronicles
      12:18 ☐
      15:1 ☐

Nehemiah 9:30 ☐

Job 32:8 ☐

Isaiah 61:1–4 ☐

Ezekiel 2:2 ☐
      11:24 ☐

Zechariah 7:12 ☐

He leads them to repentance and faith. He urges them towards righteousness and obedience. And he encourages them to respond to God's instruction and fellowship with praise and prayer.

In Psalm 51, David cried out to God about his sin. He had been convicted and brought to repentance by the Spirit. Verses 10–12 show how the Spirit alerted David to spiritual reality and drew a response from him.

Psalm 51:10–12 ☐

Isaiah 44:3–5 illustrates how the Spirit causes people to turn to God. Ezekiel 39:29 shows that the Spirit reveals God's own face to us. Ezekiel 11:19–20 & 36:25–27 make plain the difference that the Spirit makes in our lives. And Joel 2:28–32 lists some changes which take place in our lives when the Spirit comes.

Isaiah 44:3–5 ☐
Ezekiel 11:19–20 ☐
36:25–27 ☐
39:29 ☐

Joel 2:28–32 ☐

6.   He equips individuals for leadership

The Scriptures show that one of the Spirit's main Old Testament activities was equipping people for leadership.

In Genesis 41:33–42, Pharaoh chose Joseph as his leader for Egypt because he recognised that God's Spirit had given Joseph special discernment and wisdom.

Genesis
41:33–42 ☐

Numbers 11:16–29 makes it clear that the same Spirit which equipped Moses for national leadership was needed by the seventy elders for their leadership responsibilities.

Numbers
11:16–29 ☐

Judges 3:10; 6:34; 11:29; 13:25; 14:19 & 15:14 show how the Spirit enabled *judges* like Joshua, Othniel, Gideon, Jephthah and Samson to lead Israel and to deliver them from enemies.

Judges 3:10 ☐
6:34 ☐
11:29 ☐
13:25 ☐
14:19 ☐
15:14 ☐

Saul and David, the first two *kings*, were personally chosen by God as rulers – later ones merely followed the family line. 1 Samuel 10:10; 11:6; 16:13 & 19:20–23 describe how these two kings were helped by the Spirit to rule Israel effectively.

1 Samuel 10:10 ☐
11:6 ☐
16:13 ☐
19:20–23 ☐

People could only function as *prophets* if they were called, inspired and empowered by the Spirit – like Elijah, Elisha and Isaiah in 2 Kings 2:9–15; Isaiah 11:1–5 & 42:1–4. God called them into his presence to reveal his intentions to them, and also to commission and equip them with the vital resource of his Spirit.

2 Kings 2:9–15 ☐
Isaiah 11:1–5 ☐
42:1–4 ☐

7.   He equips individuals with skill and strength

Exodus 31:1–3 & 35:30–35 show how the Spirit gave Bezaleel and Oholiab all sorts of skills and abilities in craftwork to help him build a beautiful Tabernacle. Haggai 2:4–9 & Zechariah 4:6–10 show that Zerubbabel was also equipped by the Spirit to build a lovely building for God. And there is a similar equipping of Hiram in 1 Kings 7:14.

It is likely that these men were already talented workers before the Spirit came upon them. But the Spirit gave them extra-special ability in order to serve God even better.

A FORESHADOWING

Exodus 31:3 uses a phrase for receiving the Spirit that we find many times in the New Testament but which does not appear anywhere else in the Old Testament.

Many biblical truths are only partially revealed in the Old Testament: this is called a 'foreshadowing'. This means that we see the shadow in the Old Testament – the outline shape but little detail – before we come to the reality in the New Testament. We get a valuable insight into a truth in the Old Testament, and then we see the full picture in the New Testament.

We would not know the Spirit very well if we based our understanding of him only on the Old Testament. We would know that God was active through his Spirit as creator, controller, revealer, awakener and equipper. But we would not be sure that the Spirit was a distinct person. For example, Psalm 139:7 asks where we can go from God's Spirit and where we can flee from God's presence. This may suggest that the Spirit mediates God's presence, but it does not make clear the distinction of personhood between God and his Spirit.

This means that, if we only had the Old Testament, we would not necessarily think that the breath of God was any more than an extension or dimension of God, or that it was a divine person in his own right. God's triune nature is an eternal fact, but it is not fully revealed in the Old Testament.

Exodus 31:1–3 ☐
35:30–35 ☐
Haggai 2:4–9 ☐
Zechariah 4:6–10 ☐
1 Kings 7:14 ☐

Exodus 31:3 ☐

Even though we have to wait for the New Testament to make it absolutely clear that the Spirit is not just a power but also a person, there are 'foreshadowings' of his personhood in the Old Testament.

The Old Testament word-pictures about the Spirit may be rather impersonal, but they are still appropriate images for an immensely powerful being. Taken together, the pictures and the activities point us towards a person whom we see more clearly in the New Testament.

If we were to chose a modern word-picture, we could think of the Holy Spirit as the Chief Executive of the Godhead. A company's chief executive is responsible for implementing the policies, programmes, decisions and vision of the directors. So the Holy Spirit acts on the Father's behalf to implement his will.

THE HOLY SPIRIT

We have seen that there are almost 100 references to 'the Spirit' or 'the Spirit of God' in the Old Testament, but we all know that he is called 'the *Holy* Spirit' in the New Testament.

This special title is given to the Spirit only twice in the Old Testament – therefore it must have been to these two passages that John the Baptist was referring when he spoke about the *Holy* Spirit at Jesus' baptism in the Jordan.

Psalm 51

Psalm 51 is one of the seven 'penitential Psalms' and it deals powerfully with repentance. The writer – almost certainly King David – is deeply sorry for his sin and, in verse 11, he begs God for the Holy Spirit to stay with him.

If the writer's request for the 'Holy' Spirit is successful, he promises – in verses 13–15 – that he will tell sinners the way to God *and* that he will praise the Lord with his mouth.

Psalm 51 ☐

Isaiah 63

Isaiah 63:10 shows that the Holy Spirit is grieved whenever we turn away from God – this must be the exact opposite of repentance.

The whole chapter is relevant to the Holy Spirit, and it links the presence of the Holy Spirit with signs, wonders and with miraculous guidance.

Psalm 51 and Isaiah 63 – the two Old Testament references to the 'Holy' Spirit – foreshadow the Spirit's work in the New Testament. There may not be many details, but the general shape is clear.

The glorious Holy Spirit – the blowing of God – is associated with repentant lives, with sharing the good news about God, *and* with powerful signs and special direction. All that follows in the Scriptures about the Spirit merely fills in the details – for he is the same today as he was then.

Isaiah 63 □

PART TWO

the spirit in the new testament

The New Testament was written in the Greek language. The Greek word which is translated as 'Spirit' is *pneuma*, and this is another picture word.

Like the Hebrew word *ruach*, *pneuma* also carries the meaning of a powerful wind as well as a personal spirit. For example, in John 3:8, Jesus' point is appreciated all the more strongly when it is realised that *pneuma* is the word for both the wind and God's Spirit.

John 3:8 □

THE BLOWING GOD

Pneuma primarily denotes 'wind' – it comes from the Greek verb *pneo*, which means 'to blow' – but it can also mean 'breath' and 'spirit'. Like the wind, God's Spirit is invisible and powerful.

John 3:8 ☐
Revelation 11:11 ☐
Luke 8:55 ☐
       34:37–39 ☐
Acts 7:59 ☐
Hebrews 12:23 ☐
1 Corinthians
       15:45 ☐
1 Timothy 3:16 ☐
Matthew 5:3 ☐
Acts 17:16 ☐
2 Corinthians
       12:18 ☐
Ephesians 4:23 ☐
1 Corinthians
       16:18 ☐
Philemon 25 ☐
Luke 1:17 ☐
Romans 1:4 ☐
       8:25 ☐
2 Timothy 1:7 ☐
Romans 8:15 ☐
1 Corinthians
       4:21 ☐
2 Corinthians
       4:13 ☐
1 Peter 3:4 ☐
Romans 7:22 ☐
2 Corinthians
       4:16 ☐
1 Corinthians
       14:12 ☐
Revelation 1:10 ☐
       4:2 ☐
John 6:63 ☐
Romans 7:6 ☐
Matthew 8:16 ☐
1 Peter 3:19 ☐
Hebrews 1:14 ☐
Matthew 4:1 ☐
Luke 4:18 ☐

In the New Testament, *pneuma* is used incredibly widely. Here are brief examples of what the word is used to denote. It will be helpful to read these examples in several translations to get a fuller picture.

- wind – John 3:8

- breath – Revelation 11:11

- the immaterial, invisible part of humans – Luke 8:55; Acts 7:59

- the disembodied person – Luke 34:37–39; Hebrews 12;23

- the resurrection body – 1 Corinthians 15:45; 1 Timothy 3:16

- the sentient part of a person, that by which we reflect, feel, understand and desire – Matthew 5:3; Acts 17:16

- purpose or aim – 2 Corinthians 12:18; Ephesians 4:23

- the equivalent of the personal pronoun, to give emphasis and effect – 1 Corinthians 16:18; Philemon 25

- character – Luke 1:17; Romans 1:4

- moral qualities:

    – slavery – Romans 8:25

    – timidity – 2 Timothy 1:7

    – liberty – Romans 8:15

    – meekness – 1 Corinthians 4:21

    – faith – 2 Corinthians 4:13

    – quietness – 1 Peter 3:4

- the 'inner man' – Romans 7:22; 2 Corinthians 4:16

- a divine gift for service – 1 Corinthians 14:12

- vision – Revelation 1:10; 4:2

- the significance, rather than the form, of words – John 6:63; Romans 7:6

- evil spirits or demons – Matthew 8:16; 1 Peter 3:19

- angels – Hebrews 1:14

- the Holy Spirit – Matthew 4:1; Luke 4:18

We need to bear this incredible richness of *pneuma* in mind when we read about the Spirit in the New Testament. It is easy to slip into a narrow understanding of the Spirit, or to have an idea about him which is shaped by our background or experience. It is vital that we grasp the larger picture of the Spirit's nature and work.

NAMES AND TITLES

In the New Testament, the name of the Spirit is expressed in many different ways. Translated literally from the Greek, they are as follows:

- Spirit – Matthew 22:43
- Eternal Spirit – Hebrews 9:14
- the Spirit – Matthew 4:1
- Holy Spirit – Matthew 1:18
- the Holy Spirit – Matthew 28:19
- the Spirit, the Holy – Matthew 12:32
- the Spirit of promise, the Holy – Ephesians 1:13
- Spirit of God – Romans 8:9
- Spirit of the living God – 2 Corinthians 3:3
- the Spirit of God – 1 Corinthians 2:11
- the Spirit of our God – 1 Corinthians 6:11
- the Spirit of God, the Holy – Ephesians 4:30
- the Spirit of glory and of God – 1 Peter 4:14
- the Spirit of him that raised up Jesus from the dead – Romans 8:11
- the Spirit of your Father – Matthew 10:20
- the Spirit of his Son – Galatians 4:6
- Spirit of the Lord – Acts 8:39
- the Spirit of the Lord – Acts 5:9

Matthew 22:43 ☐

Hebrews 9:14 ☐

Matthew 4:1 ☐

Matthew 1:18 ☐

Matthew 28:19 ☐

Matthew 12:32 ☐

Ephesians 1:13 ☐

Romans 8:9 ☐

2 Corinthians 3:3 ☐

1 Corinthians 2:11 ☐

1 Corinthians 6:11 ☐

Ephesians 4:30 ☐

1 Peter 4:14 ☐

Romans 8:11 ☐

Matthew 10:20 ☐

Galatians 4:6 ☐

Acts 8:39 ☐

Acts 5:9 ☐

- the Lord, the Spirit – 2 Corinthians 3:18

- the Spirit of Jesus – Acts 16:7

- Spirit of Christ – Romans 8:9

- the Spirit of Jesus Christ – Philippians 1:19

- Spirit of adoption – Romans 8:15

- the Spirit of truth – John 14:17

- the Spirit of life – Romans 8:2

- the Spirit of grace – Hebrews 10:29

As we read and think about the Spirit, it is important to keep this variety of expressions in mind. It may also be right to make more use of them when we are speaking about him and talking to him.

In reading these names and titles, we may have noticed that the definite article – the word 'the' – is missing from some and present in others. This is not always translated consistently in English versions of the Bible.

In most cases, the absence of 'the' is because '*Pneuma*' is essentially a proper name – we do not write 'the Peter', 'the Jesus' or 'the God' whereas we do write 'the table', 'the breath' and 'the wind'.

We can see this in John 7:39 – which translates literally as, 'But this he spoke concerning the Spirit, whom those believing in him would receive, for Spirit was not yet given...'

As a general rule, when the New Testament uses *pneuma* to describe God's Spirit, 'the' is present when the Spirit is being distinguished from other members of the Godhead – as in John 14:26.

This means that 'Spirit' is a name which is the counterpart of 'Jesus' and 'God,' and that 'the Spirit' is a title which is the counterpart of 'the Son' and 'the Father'.

In some places, the definite article – 'the' – appears before both *pneuma* and *hagios*. This is a device which the writers use to draw our attention to the holy character of the Spirit. We can see this in Matthew 12:32; Mark 3:29; 12:36; 13:11; Luke 2:26; 10:21; John 14:26; Acts 1:16; 5:3; 7:51; 10:44; 13:2; 15:28; 19:6; 20:23, 28; 21:11; 28:25; Ephesians 4:30; Hebrews 3:7; 9:8 & 10:15.

THE PERSONAL NATURE OF THE SPIRIT

The personhood of the Spirit is emphasised by Jesus in a special way in John 14:26; 15:26; 16:8, 13 & 14.

John 14:26 ☐
15:26 ☐
16:8, 13, ☐
14 ☐

In these verses, the writer breaks the laws of grammar and uses the emphatic pronoun *ekeinos*, 'he', in the masculine, whereas the noun *pneuma* is neuter in Greek and the corresponding word in Aramaic (the language Jesus spoke) *rucha* is feminine. This was their way of stressing that the Spirit is a 'he' and not an 'it'.

This use of *ekeinos* is especially striking because in John 14:17, when the Spirit is first introduced, the grammatically correct neuter pronouns are used. This shows that the switch to the masculine in verse 26 is not a mistake but a pointer to the personality of the Spirit.

John 14:17 ☐

Some suggest that the 'he', in verse 26, refers to 'the Helper' – which is the masculine word *parakletos* in Greek. But this view underlines the fact that Jesus was introducing the Spirit as a distinctive person – as 'the Helper'.

The New Testament stress on the personality of the Spirit adds details to the Old Testament pictures of the Spirit. Jesus and the apostles clearly recognised that the person of the Spirit was active in the Old Testament, and that references to God's breath meant the Spirit's personal activity. For example:

Mark 12:36 ☐

Acts 1:16 ☐
4:25 ☐

- *Mark 12:36, Acts 1:16; & 4:25* – David is said to have spoken by the Holy Spirit in 2 Samuel 23:2

2 Samuel 23:2 ☐

- *Luke 4:18–21* – Jesus – filled with the power of the personal Holy Spirit – claims that his preaching fulfils Isaiah's witness to his own anointing by the Spirit in Isaiah 61:1–4

Luke 4:18–21 ☐

Isaiah 61:1–4 ☐

- *John 3:5–10* – Jesus rebukes Nicodemus for not realising that his teaching on the new birth of 'water and the Spirit' looks back to Ezekiel 36:25–27 & 37:1–14

John 3:5–10 ☐

Ezekiel 36:25–27 ☐
37:1–14 ☐

- *Acts 28:25; Hebrews 3:7; & 10:15–17* – Old Testament teaching with a New Testament application is ascribed to the Spirit

Acts 28:25 ☐

Hebrews 3:7 ☐
10:15–17 ☐

- *Acts 2:16–18* – Peter identifies the outpouring of the personal Spirit as that predicted in Joel 2:28–29

Acts 2:16–18 ☐

Joel 2:28–29 ☐

In the New Testament, the Holy Spirit is clearly introduced as the third member of the Trinity. It is plain that he is both fully personal *and* fully divine.

If 'the Holy Spirit' was merely a way of describing God's power, the New Testament would not continually name the Spirit as a 'him' rather than as an 'it'. It would not show him acting in such a thoroughly personal manner. For example, the New Testament reveals that the Holy Spirit hears, speaks, helps, witnesses, convinces, convicts, commands, tells, declares, leads, guides, grieves, teaches, forbids, opposes, desires, and gives speech.

It could be argued that grieving the Spirit simply means grieving God. Yet it is unlikely that he could do *all* these things if he were not a person in his own right. However, the Spirit also intercedes with the Father for believers. It would be impossible for him to intercede if he was merely an extension of God, so it is the Spirit's ministry of intercession which conclusively proves his distinctive personhood.

On top of all this, if 'the Holy Spirit' was just another way of describing God's presence, the New Testament would not make it so clear that he is God, yet distinct from 'the Father' and 'the Son'.

Passages like Matthew 28:19; Acts 5:3–4; 1 Corinthians 12:4–6; 2 Corinthians 13:14; Ephesians 1:3–14; 2:18; 3:14–19; 4:4–6; 2 Thessalonians 2:13–14; 1 Peter 1:2; & Revelation 1:4–5 link the Father, the Son and the Spirit together in a way which leaves no room for doubt: the Spirit really is Almighty God.

JOHN'S ANNOUNCEMENT

Anybody who knows nothing about Jesus, who turns to the Gospels for information, is faced with John the Baptist's announcement that Jesus 'will baptise you with Holy Spirit and fire'. This is recorded at the beginning of each gospel: Matthew 3:1–12; Mark 1:1–8; Luke 3:1–18 & John 1:19–34.

As far as John seems to have been concerned, the single most important task Jesus would perform would be to baptise in Holy Spirit and fire.

John drew a parallel between his baptising in water and the Stronger One's baptising in Spirit and fire. Just as the crowds were immersed in water by John, so Jesus' followers would be immersed in Holy Spirit and fire.

This must have reminded John's listeners – who knew the Scriptures so well – of the Old Testament pictures about God's Spirit and, in particular, of Psalm 51 and Isaiah 63.

But the people who heard John may have been challenged by the mention of a baptism in fire. They would have known passages like Isaiah 1:25; 4:3–6; Daniel 7:10; Zechariah 13:9 & Malachi 3:2–3 which describe the Spirit coming in judgement to purge people's lives.

Isaiah 1:25 ☐

Daniel 7:10 ☐

Zechariah 13:9 ☐

Malachi 3:2–3 ☐

Isaiah 4:3–6 ☐

All this suggests that, while John's baptism can wash, Jesus' will purify us now to save us from the judgement. John's baptism in water may 'wipe the slate clean', but Jesus' baptism in Spirit and fire promises to transform the very slate.

LUKE'S SPECIAL PHRASE

We have seen that Exodus 31:3 describes Bezaleel as being 'filled with the Spirit'. Luke uses the same phrase again and again in both his Gospel and in Acts – which he also wrote.

Exodus 31:3 ☐

Luke uses the phrase to describe what happened to ordinary people like Elizabeth and Zachariah – Luke 1:41, 67 – as well as to people like John and Jesus – Luke 1:15; 4:1. He uses the same expression a further seven times in Acts 2:4; 4:8; 6:5; 7:55; 9:17; 11:23 & 13:52.

Luke 1:41 ☐
1: 67 ☐
1:15 ☐
4:1 ☐

Acts 2:4 ☐
4:8 ☐
6:5 ☐
7:55 ☐
9:17 ☐
11:23 ☐
13:52 ☐

The Greek word Luke uses for 'to fill' is *pletho*. This is the Greek word which is used in Matthew 27:48 and John 19:29 to describe the way a sponge was filled with sour wine for Jesus.

At the cross, a dry sponge was immersed in a jar which was full of wine. The wine was not poured into the sponge; instead the sponge was filled by being placed into the wine. This is how we are filled with Holy Spirit.

Matthew 27:48 ☐

John 19:29 ☐

We do not contain the Spirit. Instead, we are plunged by Jesus into Holy Spirit to be filled like a sponge being filled with liquid. We are saturated by the Spirit, we are filled with the Spirit, because we are placed *into* the Spirit to start living in the presence of the Spirit.

Luke uses the same phrase to describe *both* the experience of becoming filled *and* the result of being filled – Luke 1:41 & 4:1; Acts 2:4 & 4:8. This means that we remain filled with Spirit for as long as we remain living in Spirit.

JESUS' MINISTRY

The Gospels show that Jesus' life was lived in the Holy Spirit from his first moments on earth. Matthew 1:18–21 and Luke 1:31–35 show how Jesus was conceived by the Holy Spirit with the intention that he would be holy and God's own Son.

Although Jesus was fully divine, he did not cling to his equality with God. Philippians 2:5–11 shows that he emptied himself. He laid aside his majesty and picked up humility. He chose not to exercise his omnipotence and omniscience and put on all the human weaknesses except sin.

He did not cease to be God – because he could not give up his divine nature – rather he sacrificed the public treatment and honour due to him because he was God and assumed the condition of a slave. And it was exactly because he had taken on humanity in this way, that Jesus needed to be filled with Spirit before he could begin his ministry.

Jesus' baptism by John was the moment of his commissioning and equipping for ministry. As he rose from the river, Matthew 3:13–17 reports that the Spirit came down like a dove and that the Father announced, 'This is my beloved Son, in whom I am well pleased'.

This was Jesus' anointing and equipping for service. Mark 1:12–13 shows that the first act of the Spirit was to drive Jesus into the desert for a dramatic battle with the evil one. Luke 4:1 states that Jesus was 'filled with Holy Spirit' when he entered the wilderness, but Luke 4:14 reports that he was 'full of the power of the Spirit' when he left the wilderness.

There is a critical difference between being filled with the Holy Spirit and being full of the power of the Spirit. The former is the basic condition. The latter is the result of the condition being lived out in obedience and overcoming temptation. Jesus' spiritual purity in the face of demonic temptation resulted in his spiritual power.

Luke 4:16–27 describes how Jesus went from the wilderness to the Nazareth synagogue, quoted from Isaiah 61, and applied it to himself. At the river, he had been anointed to serve. Acts 10:38 reflects on this anointing and states that – once and for all – God became 'with him'.

Luke 4:16–27 ☐

Isaiah 61 ☐

Acts 10:38 ☐

Because of his anointing with the Spirit, Jesus was enabled to do that which – as a man – he had previously been unable to do. He 'went about doing good and healing all who were oppressed by the devil'.

The whole of Jesus' ministry was shot through with the Spirit. The Holy Spirit was the source of his life, his power and his emotions.

- He was filled with joy by the Spirit, Luke 10:21

- He drove out demons by the Spirit, Matthew 12:28

- He taught by the Spirit, Acts 1:2

- He sacrificed himself by the Spirit, Hebrews 9:14

Luke 10:21 ☐

Matthew 12:28 ☐

Acts 1:2 ☐

Hebrews 9:14 ☐

We can say that Jesus' life, growth, character, emotions and ministry were all the result of his being born of the Spirit, his being filled with the Holy Spirit, and his continued living in the Spirit.

THE PARAKLETOS

The New Testament records that Jesus taught little about the Spirit until the Last Supper – John 13–17. At that farewell meal, Jesus explained it was to the apostles' advantage that he left. In John 16:7, Jesus said that the *Parakletos* would not come unless he departed.

John 16:7 ☐

14:16 ☐

Jesus referred five times to the Spirit as the '*Parakletos*' during the Last Supper. In John 14:16, he used the Greek word *allos* for 'another'. By using *allos* instead of *heteros*, Jesus underlines the fact that the Spirit is 'another the same as', not 'another different to', Jesus.

It is hard to translate *Parakletos* into English. Most versions of the Bible use a different word: for example, Counsellor, Advocate, Helper, Comforter or Encourager.

The word comes from *parakaleo* – which means 'to call alongside'. This shows that the Holy Spirit is called alongside us, and that he calls from alongside us. He comes alongside to help us, to speak for us, to comfort, encourage and advise us. He helps in the same way as Jesus!

John 14:25–27 □
15:26 □
16:7–11 □
16:13 □
16:14–15 □

John 14:25–27 reveals him as teacher; 15:26 states that he will bear witness to Jesus; 16:7–11 points to his important activity in the world – convincing it about sin, righteousness and judgement; and 16:13 promises that the Spirit will lead disciples into complete truth.

The essence of the Spirit's work is revealed in John 16:14–15. There, Jesus explains that the Spirit 'will glorify me'. Everything the Spirit says and does is to glorify, to illuminate, to floodlight, to focus the world's attention on Jesus. Please note that his ministry is aimed at *the world*, not the church: this is a vital principle for us to grasp.

The Holy Spirit never draws attention to himself. He always remains in the background, ensuring that all glory and attention goes to Jesus. When we are filled with the Holy Spirit, we will surely behave like him.

THE BEGINNING OF THE CHURCH

John 20:20–22 □

Genesis 2:7 □

Ezekiel 37:5–9 □

Jesus' introduction to the *Parakletos* was his last message to his apostles. He then left for Calvary. Three days later, he burst from the tomb and walked through locked doors to thrill his followers. His first words to the disciples, in John 20:20–22, and are rather like Genesis 2:7 and Ezekiel 37:5–9: ' "Peace to you! As the Father has sent me, I also send you." And when he had said this he breathed on them, and said to them, "Receive the Holy Spirit." '

Jesus' breathing or blowing on them appears to have been a prophetic action which was fulfilled at Pentecost when the Spirit came in a rushing wind. Just as Jesus had had to wait until his baptism for God's Spirit, so the church now had to wait until Pentecost for the Spirit.

Jesus' last words before Gethsemane, his first words to the disciples after the resurrection, and his last words before his ascension, were all about the Holy Spirit. In Acts 1:1–8, he reminded the disciples about John's announcement; and – just before ascending – he promised that they would receive power when the Holy Spirit came upon them.

Acts 1:1–8 ☐

PENTECOST

In New Testament days, the feast of Pentecost celebrated the end of the first phase of the harvest. The first fruits had been picked. The latter rain had fallen. Jews looked forward to three dry, hot, hard-working months of summer when they would reap the harvest.

When we understand this, we can grasp why God chose Pentecost to empower the Church. It was time for harvest, and they needed the Spirit's help to gather it in.

Acts 2:1–41 tells the story of Pentecost. Jesus had told the disciples to stay in Jerusalem until they received the promised power. They obeyed, and Jesus kept his promise.

Acts 2:1–41 ☐

At Pentecost:

- the room was the baptistery

- the disciples were the candidates

- Jesus was the baptiser

- the Holy Spirit was the element

- 'and they were all filled with Holy Spirit' was the result

The fire

The tongues of fire which appeared at Pentecost were a startling reminder of the first Temple's consecration in 2 Chronicles 7:1–3. God's fire fell then and showed that God had come to live in an earthly home. This was what happened again at Pentecost.

2 Chronicles 7:1–3 ☐

On the day of Pentecost, the Spirit came as holy fire and God's new temple – the church – was purified, dedicated, surrounded by glory and filled with God's power and presence.

God had led the people of Israel through the wilderness in the form of a pillar of fire. Jesus had promised that the *Parakletos* would lead the disciples. So the Spirit came as fire to guide the church.

God had revealed his presence and his character through fire which had blazed in a bush but not consumed it. He had then given Moses a commission which took him the rest of his life to fulfil.

So the Spirit came as fire at Pentecost to reveal the presence and character of God, and to commission the church with a task which it would take to the end of time to perform.

Holy fire had purified Isaiah's lips and provided him with words to speak to the people. So the church received the gift of Spirit-inspired speech to witness to Jesus – just as Jesus had promised. The *Parakletos* had been called alongside to help the disciples to witness.

The wind

The sound of the mighty rushing wind at Pentecost revealed that God was blowing again.

The violent wind of God had been active in creation. He had dried the waters of the flood to usher in a new age. He had divided the Red Sea to allow the Jews to enter the new land of promise. He had created a mighty army out of a valley of dry bones.

The hurricane of God's Spirit now blew into the church. He came alongside to breath energy and power, to bring new order and turn raw recruits into an army.

The result

Acts 2:4 □

Acts 2:4 shows the first result was that the disciples 'were all filled with Holy Spirit and began to speak in other tongues, as the Spirit gave them utterance'.

Peter then stood before the crowd of Jews and explained that what had happened was what had been prophesied by Joel. God had poured his Spirit upon them.

However Pentecost was the day of *first* fruits. This was the first instalment, not the total package. The harvest of God's Spirit had begun, but it was far from over.

Peter did not claim that Joel's prophecy had been completely fulfilled. He merely explained that it was what Joel had spoken about. Joel 2:28–32 was fulfilled only in the experience of the people who were actually present at Pentecost. However the possibility of the prophecy being fulfilled in the experience of all humanity came into being. The Spirit's coming was just the first fruit. There was much more to come.

Joel 2:28–32 ☐

Jesus proclaimed

Once Peter had finished quoting from Joel, he launched into the first Pentecost sermon. 'Men of Israel, hear these words: Jesus of Nazareth...' With the Spirit's help, Peter preached about Jesus. Three thousand people responded – this was the difference that the Spirit made.

At Pentecost, the risen Christ did what John the Baptist had promised he would do. He baptised in Holy Spirit and fire. The outpouring of the Spirit showed that Jesus had ascended and taken his place at the Father's right hand. It proved that Jesus was alive!

Pentecost was the incarnation of the Spirit into the church. Through the Spirit's coming, the church could become all that Christ would have his body become on earth.

THE AGE OF THE SPIRIT

Since Pentecost, we have been living in 'the Age of the Spirit'. This is quite different from the period before Pentecost that we read about in the Old Testament. One of the main differences is the total availability of the Holy Spirit for all people who serve God.

Until Pentecost, the Spirit was given to only a special few believers – mainly to prophets, judges and some kings. Numbers 11:16–30 describes how Moses needed help, but his burden could only be shared with the seventy elders on whom the Spirit came.

Numbers
11:16–30 ☐

Joel 2:28–29 ☐

In verse 29, Moses exclaimed, 'Oh that all the Lord's people were prophets and that the Lord would put his Spirit upon them'. Joel 2:28–29 looked forward to a day when God would do exactly that. God kept his promise at Pentecost when he poured out his Spirit *without restriction* upon the church.

At Pentecost, there was no limitation on the giving of the Spirit by God, and no restriction on the receiving of the Spirit by men and women.

Since then, right through the 'Age of the Spirit', every Christian believer has been able to receive Holy Spirit. Every aspect of the Spirit's character and power that we have read about in the Old and the New Testaments have always been available to every believer.

Continuous witness

The 'Age of the Spirit' is characterised by the Spirit's witness to Jesus. Since Pentecost, the Spirit has continuously borne witness to Jesus, has given glory to Jesus, and has focused the world's attention on the only Son of God.

The witnessing Spirit acts as humanity's prosecutor, causing people to admit that they are wrong, guilty, in need of forgiveness. He works in people's lives, bringing home the enormity of rejecting Jesus – or not taking him seriously enough.

The Spirit's way of convincing and convicting people is through Christian preaching, evangelism, witnessing, loving good works, missionary activity, church planting, prayer, intercession, and so on. As witnessing Christians depend on him, he applies to individual minds the truths that the Christians are proclaiming about Jesus.

Holy lifestyle

We have seen that water is an important biblical picture of the Spirit. Water *always* seeks out the lowest place. So the Holy Spirit is *always* self-effacing. Throughout the New Testament, instead of drawing attention to himself, he always points people to the Son and to the Father. This holy humility is an important characteristic of those people who are truly controlled by the Holy Spirit.

In Galatians 5:16–26, Paul contrasts 'the works of the flesh' with 'the fruit of the Spirit'. He shows that the lifestyle of those who are led by the Spirit in his Age is 'love, joy, peace, long-suffering, kindness, goodness, faithfulness, gentleness and self-control'.

Paul makes plain that 'hatred, contentions, jealousies, outbursts of wrath, selfish ambitions, dissensions and envy' are fundamentally opposed to the Spirit.

In John 14:26, Jesus promised that the Spirit would be sent 'in my name'. He is Jesus' spokesman and personal representative. He stays with disciples and draws people into a partnership which embraces faith, hope, love, obedience, adoration and commitment to Christ.

| Galatians |
| 5:16–26 ☐ |

| John 14:26 ☐ |
| 16:13 ☐ |

Basic truth

In John 14:26, Jesus taught that the *parakletos* would 'teach you all things, and bring to your remembrance all things that I said to you'. In John 16:13, he also said that the Spirit of truth would guide his followers into all truth.

Ever since the day of Pentecost, the Spirit has been acting as the church's teacher – gently guiding us towards the truth. In fact the whole of the Scriptures has been 'breathed' for us.

The Spirit's way of teaching is to make us recall and understand what Jesus said. Jesus' 'alls' in John 14:26 & 16:13 do not mean that the Spirit will teach us all there is to know about anything and everything'. Instead, they mean he will teach 'all we need to know about Jesus'.

Equally, 'the things to come' means what is before Jesus – the cross, resurrection, reign, return and restoration – not what is before us. We must remember that the Spirit always points us to Jesus.

Spiritual gifts

When Moses longed for all God's people to prophesy, he was yearning for the Spirit to enable God's people to function at a higher – a *super*natural – level.

This is precisely what the Spirit has been doing since Pentecost. He has given 'gifts' to God's people which have helped them to carry out the task of establishing God's kingdom.

Romans 12:3–13 ☐

1 Corinthians
      12:1–11 ☐

Ephesians 4:1–13 ☐

The New Testament describes these gifts in different ways. However, Romans 12:3–13, 1 Corinthians 12:1–11 and Ephesians 4:1–13 show that 'spiritual gifts' are given to help *all* of God's people to witness, to worship and to work for God's kingdom. These gifts are not reserved for a few. They are tools to help all believers get the job done! We will look at these in a later section.

Constant change

We must never forget that the Spirit is not only lowly water, he is also the wind – the blowing – of God. He is that holy hurricane which we can neither predict nor control. We may know that he is God's power in *action*, but we must recognise this means that he will often introduce surprising new developments.

The book of Acts lists some major changes which were brought by the Spirit: the amazing events of Pentecost; Peter's struggle to enter Cornelius' house; Paul's pioneering journeys.

Paul's letters show how the Spirit of truth changed Jewish believers' ideas about Gentiles, circumcision, faith and grace. And so through the centuries – right up to today – the church has struggled to keep in step with the Spirit, as he goes on urging us to accept new ways of showing God's love and to embrace fresh structures which are more relevant to our culture.

Christ's presence

John 14:21–23 ☐

John 14:21–23 is pivotal in our understanding of the New Testament teaching about the Spirit. It is his work to make the presence of Christ – and fellowship with him and the Father – a real experience for all those who show that they love Jesus by obeying his words.

The Spirit reveals Jesus to us. He draws us into Christ's presence and helps us to live in fellowship with him. The New Testament makes it plain that the Holy Spirit's fundamental ministry is to glorify or floodlight Jesus in this way.

He has been sent to stand alongside us and say, 'Look at Jesus; listen to him; receive his love; enjoy his life; get to know him better; taste his joy and peace'. His role is simply to bring us and Christ together and to ensure that we stay together – for all eternity.

PART THREE

the spirit and jesus

By introducing the Holy Spirit in John 14:15–18 as *allos parakletos*, Jesus made it plain that the Helper/Comforter/Encourager/Advocate would be 'another the same' as himself. Because the Spirit is *allos* Jesus, we can see the nature and character of the Spirit when we look at Jesus. If we really want to know what the Spirit is like, we have only to look at the biblical records about Jesus.

John 14:15–18 ☐

But although Jesus was and is fully God, he was and is also the Ideal Human Being. This means that, when we look at Jesus, we also see what we are meant to be like. Every one of Christ's words and actions reveal how ordinary men and women should live.

As the Ideal Person, Jesus depended completely on the Holy Spirit. Jesus was filled with the Spirit, and he lived in fellowship – or partnership – with the Spirit. In his earthly life and ministry, Jesus relied entirely on the initiative, direction and power of the Holy Spirit.

This means that, in the Gospels' portrayal of Jesus' life and ministry, not only do we have a perfect picture of the Spirit's nature and character, we also have the perfect example of the partnership we are meant to have with the Spirit.

THE ANOINTED

Throughout the world, Jesus is known by the title *The Christ*. This is derived from the Greek word *Christos*, which means 'anointed'. *Christos* has exactly the same meaning as the Hebrew word *Messiah*. To say that Jesus is 'the Messiah' is no different from saying that he is 'the Christ'. Both titles identify Jesus as 'the Anointed One'.

Luke 4:18–21 ☐

Mark 8:29 ☐

Acts 10:38 ☐

Jesus claimed to be anointed in Luke 4:18–21; and Peter recognised Jesus as the Christ, the Anointed, in Mark 8:29 and Acts 10:38. It is clear from these verses that the anointing is the Holy Spirit and that the purpose of the anointing is service.

We have seen that, in the Old Testament, prophets, priests, kings and holy objects were anointed with holy oil as an act of consecration to God and in dedication for serving God.

In the New Testament, the symbolic anointing with inanimate holy oil was transformed into the spiritual reality of anointing with a person, with Holy Spirit.

This anointing still consecrates the person to God and dedicates them for service, but it also goes much further. The anointing with Holy Spirit equips believers with the power that they need to perform their God-given task of service.

Jesus' anointing

Jesus did not become *The Christ* when he was anointed with the Spirit at his baptism, for he had been the Christ at the Father's right hand in the heavenlies from before the beginning of time. Rather, Jesus' anointing with the Spirit at the Jordan openly declared who he was – in the same way that the Father's words at the baptism revealed him as the Son and did not make him the Son.

Matthew 1:18–21 ☐

Luke 1:31–35 ☐

However, Jesus' anointing with the Spirit did consecrate and equip him to serve as *The Christ*. We have already seen that Jesus' earthly life was lived in the Spirit from before he was born. Matthew 1:18–21 and Luke 1:31–35 show that he was conceived by the Spirit to be holy.

Although Jesus had been born of the Spirit, he needed to be anointed with the Spirit before he could begin his ministry. Jesus' baptism was his commissioning and equipping for service. It was his moment of visible, public consecration to God's work. Leaving everything behind, Jesus walked into the river, put himself unconditionally at the disposal of the Father, and was baptised in dependence on God to reveal the next step in his life.

John 1:32–34 testifies that, as Jesus came out of the river, the Spirit came down like a dove and rested on him.

John 1:32–34 ☐

Matthew 3:13–17 ☐

Mark 1:9–11 ☐

Luke 3:21–22 ☐

Matthew 3:13–17; Mark 1:9–11 & Luke 3:21–22 also describe Jesus' anointing with the Spirit. In that moment, Jesus became the bearer of the Spirit so that he might become the baptiser in the Spirit.

The effects of Jesus' anointing

John 3:34 shows that Jesus' anointing was unlimited. As a result, he has became known as *Jesus Christ* – which is, *Jesus the Anointed*. From the moment of his anointing with the Spirit onwards, people were amazed by Jesus: he was 'not as other men'.

John 3:34 ☐

Matthew 4:1 ☐

Mark 1:12 ☐

Matthew 4:1 and Mark 1:12 show that the first consequence for Jesus of his anointing was to be driven by the Spirit into the desert to do battle with the devil. His anointing meant that he had to face temptations.

Luke 4:1 portrays Jesus as 'filled with Holy Spirit' when he entered the wilderness. After his struggle with Satan, Luke describes Jesus in 4:14 as returning to Galilee 'full of the power of the Spirit'.

Luke 4:1 ☐

4:14 ☐

4:16–27 ☐

Luke 4:16–27 shows that Jesus went directly to Nazareth. He read from Isaiah 61 and applied it to himself. He claimed that the Spirit was upon him because he had been anointed. Now he had the anointing – the vital help of the Spirit – to preach, to heal, to bring freedom.

Acts 10:38 shows that, through the anointing, 'God was with' Jesus. In the Spirit, he could now do as a man what before he had been unable to do in his humanity. He could heal 'all who were oppressed by the devil'.

Acts 10:38 ☐

How was this possible? Simply, because God the Holy Spirit was with him in a new way. They were in fellowship – in partnership. The *Parakletos* had been 'called alongside' to help, direct and empower Jesus in his humanity.

JESUS' MODEL MINISTRY

If Jesus needed the anointing of the Spirit for his ministry on earth, how much more must we need the same anointing to reach people with the Good News of God's love!

Acts 1:8 ☐

Romans 8:11 ☐

Isaiah 61:1–2 ☐

Luke 4:18–19 ☐

Thank God, Acts 1:8 and Romans 8:11 promise that exactly the same Holy Spirit anointing which rested on Jesus is promised to us. Jesus was anointed to do the things listed in Isaiah 61:1–2 and Luke 4:18–19. Exactly the same work still needs to be done today, and the same anointing is available to all believers.

We know that – as the Ideal Human Being – Jesus is our example in all things. We are called to obey the Father as Jesus obeyed the Father; to depend on the Spirit as Jesus depended on the Spirit; to love and serve the people around us as Jesus did – and so on.

But more than that, we are meant to share Jesus' ministry. Christ's ministry is the model for all ministry. If we want to minister in the power of the Spirit, we should look at Jesus. He is the great Servant Minister who perfectly ministered in the full power and demonstration of the Spirit.

Jesus' ministry seems to have had four great themes or purposes which are emphasised in each of the four Gospels.

1.   He came to break the power of evil and death

In his ministry, in the power of the Spirit, Jesus:

- established the kingdom of heaven

- disarmed the evil powers of darkness

- preached a gospel of repentance

- taught his followers about judgement

- gave them clear guidelines for behaviour

In short, Jesus was a mighty king who was concerned to found a kingdom. He ruled over nature and conquered demons. He healed lepers and revived the dead. Devils feared him. Storms obeyed him. But God's people of Israel would not receive their king.

If Jesus is our model ministry, it means something of his kingly authority should be seen in us. We will confront evil powers. We will be face to face with disease. We will preach a message of repentance, judgement and obedience. We will remind people of Jesus' commands. But we will only share his royal effectiveness when we share his Holy Spirit anointing!

2. He came to seek and to save the lost

Through his ministry, Jesus showed himself to be the suffering servant of Isaiah 53 who comes to serve and to offer himself as a sacrifice.

Isaiah 53 ☐

Mark 10:45 shows that Jesus came 'not to be served but to serve, and to give his life as a ransom for many'. In Mark 10:21, he called others not only to follow him but also 'to take up the cross'. Together with the Spirit, Jesus came:

Mark 10:45 ☐
10:21 ☐

- to save lost, needy people who were powerless to save themselves

- to make atonement for the sins of all humanity

- to act as a substitute for every man, woman and child

- to bear God's wrath against sin

The whole of Jesus' earthly ministry was coloured by the cross. It is impossible to separate Jesus' teaching and healing ministry from the suffering and rejection that he endured.

All this means that when we model our lives and ministries on Christ we will willingly embrace service, sacrifice and suffering. Passages like Philippians 2:5–8 come alive when we realise that we follow God's suffering servant.

Philippians 2:5–8 ☐

We must not forget that the anointing is the humble, gentle, self-effacing Holy Spirit. We should not seek for power unless we are prepared to embrace lowly service and Christ-like suffering.

3. He came to show a life of perfect consecration to the Father

Jesus was not just a king and a servant, he was also the ideal human being, the perfect example of humanity, the pattern life for all humankind.

In his ministry – as a man filled with the Spirit – Jesus:

- was tested in every possible way

- was subject to ordinary conflict and emotions, yet remained without sin

- was the sympathetic friend of sinners and a man to be followed

- was on the side of the lowest members of society

- constantly warned about the dangers of wealth and demanded generosity in his followers

- stressed the need for forgiveness, urging people to forgive others and practising this himself on the cross

This shows that our everyday lives really matter. We cannot separate ministry from morals. Jesus' power and purity were equal evidences of his anointing. If we model ourselves on Christ we will live with his holiness – as well as healing with his authority and serving with his compassion.

4.   He came to show what God is like

Jesus also came as God's living Word, as a unique and complete revelation of the invisible God – Father, Son and Spirit, to reproduce the divine nature and character in ordinary men and women.

Jesus' spirit-filled, directed and empowered ministry:

- orders us to obey the king

- invites us to allow the servant to serve us

- asks us to follow the perfect man

- dazzles us with life, light, love, truth and glory – so that we will love and believe in God's glorious, light-bearing, life-bringing Son

Everywhere Jesus went, in everything he said and did, he revealed the presence of God. Jesus emphasised his oneness with the Father and explained that his words and deeds were the very words and deeds of the Father. When people looked and listened to Jesus, they saw God. When we look at Jesus, we can also see God. Through Christ, we know what the Father is like, what the Spirit is like – and what we can and should be like.

In a similar way, our Spirit-filled, directed and empowered lives and ministries should also point people to the Father. The Spirit is God, and when we are filled with the Spirit – when we are in him and he is in us – we radiate the presence of God.

THE DISCIPLER

Jesus spent about three years in earthly ministry. He used this time to train the disciples in ministry so that they could carry on his work after he had returned to heaven and the *Parakletos* had come in his place.

There was an inner group of twelve apostles who travelled with Jesus and were deeply involved with him in his ministry. Matthew 10, Mark 6:7–13 and Luke 9:1–6 describe how the twelve were sent out in pairs to live and minister in the same way as Jesus. In these passages, Jesus instructed them how they should minister and how they should behave.

Matthew 10 ☐

Mark 6:7–13 ☐

Luke 9:1–6 ☐

10:1–23 ☐

Matthew
28:19–20 ☐

Luke 10:1–23 reports that 72 others were sent out to live and minister in pairs. Jesus instructed them to live simply, preach and heal.

Finally, just before his ascension, Matthew 28:19–20 reports how Jesus told *all* his disciples to make and mature more disciples. This commission was entrusted not just to the generation of his day, but to all generations – to us. We can do this only if we share Christ's anointing. We need to live as the Anointed One did – in the presence of the Spirit, depending on the Spirit for strength and guidance.

JESUS' EARTHLY MINISTRY

After his anointing, Jesus spent three years preaching, teaching and healing. We have seen that Jesus offers us exactly the same anointing as he had, that he calls us to carry out the same work he did, and that his balanced ministry is the perfect model for us today. However we must also grasp and apply four basic principles which undergirded Jesus' earthly ministry.

1.   Jesus ministered with prayer

Jesus was a man of prayer. He rose early to pray and remained awake late to pray. We can see him in prayer at every stage of his ministry. He prayed:

Luke 3:21 ☐

- at his baptism, Luke 3:21

Mark 1:35 ☐
6:46 ☐

- after much ministry, Mark 1:35; 6:46; Luke 5:16

Luke 5:16 ☐
6:12 ☐

- for a complete night before selecting the inner group of twelve disciples, Luke 6:12

9:18 ☐

- when revealing himself as the Anointed One of God, Luke 9:18

9:28–29 ☐

- alone in the presence of his disciples, Luke 9:28–29

John 17 ☐

- at the last supper, John 17

Luke 22:41 ☐

- in Gethsemane, Luke 22:41, Mark 14:32

Mark 14:32 ☐

Luke 23:34 ☐

- at the crucifixion, Luke 23:34

24:30 ☐

- after his resurrection, Luke 24:30

Prayer was a secret of Jesus' dynamic ministry. If we want to follow him, intercessory prayer will dominate our ministries too. There is much about this in the *Sword of the Spirit* book, *Effective Prayer*.

2.   He ministered with obedience

John 5:19 ☐
5:30 ☐
6:38 ☐
7:28–29 ☐
8:26 ☐
8:28–29 ☐
10:18 ☐
12:49–50 ☐

John 5:19, 30; 6:38; 7:28–29; 8:26, 28–29; 10:18 & 12:49–50 are an extraordinary series of sayings. Time and again, Jesus stated that he himself could do nothing by himself.

Acts 2:22 ☐

By a massive effort of self-denial, Jesus restricted himself to saying, doing and going what and where the Father told him through the Spirit. Acts 2:22 makes it clear that *God* performed the miracles *through* Jesus. This means that miracles did not happen because Jesus was divine, but because he was filled with the Spirit and living in obedience to the Father through the Spirit.

We know that we are meant to obey God and that the devil tempts us to do the opposite:

- to *disobey* God's command

- to *presume* to do something he has not commanded

Both actions are sinful. Jesus never disobeyed God, and never acted or spoke without first knowing God's prompting through the Spirit.

In the temptations, Jesus was urged to act independently of the Spirit's prompting and work a miracle without any instructions. The devil tempted him to move from a natural desire for food, power and prestige to a sinful presumption to satisfy those desires without the Spirit's prompting.

Jesus was not tempted to perform evil deeds, but to do his own deeds – to act without the Spirit's prompting. However, the ideal human being never did anything on his own initiative: he only did the few things that the Father told him through the Spirit.

3.   Jesus ministered with compassion

Jesus ministered not to attract attention to himself, but because he loved needy people and cared about their needs. Compassion drove Jesus to give people his time, his love, his energy, his life – his all.

Mark 1:41 records Jesus' compassion for one leper. Mark 6:34 reveals his compassion for a vast crowd of needy people. And Mark 10:21 describes Jesus' compassionate feelings towards the wealthy aristocrat who would not become a follower.

Mark 1:41 ☐
6:34 ☐
10:21 ☐

4.   Jesus ministered with the Spirit's help

We have seen that Jesus' anointing with the Spirit made all the difference. Passages like John 5:19 and John 14:10 show us that Jesus restricted himself to saying and doing what the Father instructed.

John 5:19 ☐
14:10 ☐

Jesus' ministry was based entirely on his relationship with the Father and the Spirit. He did only what the Father was doing – and the Spirit helped him to carry this out.

However, Jesus did not minister only through the anointing of the Spirit and according to the Father's will, he also ministered through the gifts that the Spirit gave him – precisely the same ones that the Spirit gives us today.

Jesus had tremendous skill in ministering according to the gifts of the Spirit. In fact, we see all the New Testament gifts in Jesus' ministry except tongues and interpretation.

Mark 11:20–25 ☐

John 11:41–42 ☐

Mark 6:30–52 ☐

John 2:1–11 ☐

Matthew 4:23–25 ☐

Mark 5:21–43 ☐

Luke 13:10–17 ☐

Matthew
      16:17–23 ☐

John 2:19 ☐
      1:47–50 ☐
      4:16–20 ☐

For example, we can see Jesus using:

- the gift of faith – Mark 11:20–25 & John 11:41–42

- the gift of miracles – Mark 6:30–52 & John 2:1–11

- the gift of healing – Matthew 4:23–25 & Mark 5:21–43

- the word of wisdom – Luke 13:10–17

- the discerning of spirits – Matthew 16:17–23

- the gift of prophecy – John 2:19

- the word of knowledge – John 1:47–50 & John 4:16–20

It is important we grasp the truth that Jesus did not depend on a pattern or formula when he was ministering – he depended on the help and prompting of the Spirit.

When we read the Gospels we see that Jesus ministered differently on almost every occasion. Sometimes he touched people, sometimes he did not. Sometimes he spoke healing commands, sometimes he did not. Sometimes he made the person do something, sometimes he did not.

Jesus never ministered according to his experience. Instead, he always ministered by obeying the Father and depending on the Spirit – and that usually meant something different for each person he helped.

JESUS' MINISTRY TODAY

Matthew
      28:18–20 ☐

Mark 16:15–18 ☐

Luke 24:44–49 ☐

Acts 3:6 ☐
      5:12–16 ☐
      8:4–8 ☐
      9:32–43 ☐
      16:6–10 ☐

Jesus' ministry did not end at the cross. The Gospels record the start of Jesus' ministry, not the total of his ministry.

Matthew 28:18–20, Mark 16:15–18 and Luke 24:44–49 describe Jesus' charge to his disciples to continue his ministry on earth – and his promise to carry on working with them.

Acts shows how Jesus worked through the first Christians – through the church. We can see how Jesus' ministry develops in: Acts 3:6; 5:12–16; 8:4–8; 9:32–43 & 16:6–10.

All kinds of signs, wonders and healings were performed through the apostles – with many people turning to Jesus. Leaders were guided by the Spirit to go to specific places to preach the good news. The gospel was preached everywhere, and was confirmed by many miracles – even by people being raised from the dead.

Jesus has carried on ministering like this to the needy people of our world right down through the centuries. It is now our responsibility to continue the same work that we read about in the New Testament.

However, we do not have to do this on our own – in our own strength and ability – for there are four vital things that Jesus does to help us minister.

1. He prays for us

We have seen that prayer was one of the secrets of Jesus' dynamic ministry. Romans 8:34 and Hebrews 7:25 show that it still is!

Romans 8:34 ☐

Hebrews 7:25 ☐

These two verses reveal the present heavenly ministry of Jesus. Wherever we are, whatever we are doing, Jesus Christ is at the right hand of the Father praying for us to carry out his ministry in the manner that he expects!

2. He provides the resources

Jesus has not left us empty-handed in the face of an overwhelmingly strong enemy. He has disarmed and defeated the forces of darkness, and given us the same anointing that he had to carry out his works.

But Ephesians 4:11–12 shows us that Jesus has done even more by giving gifts for the equipping of the saints for the work of ministry.

Ephesians 4:11–12 ☐

These spiritual gifts are leadership roles in the church. Some local congregations read this scripture and expect their minister to fulfil all the leadership roles and do all the ministry himself. These important gifts have been given to the church by Jesus so that *every* member can begin to minister in the power of the Spirit.

- *Apostles* (the word literally means *one who is sent*) are pioneers who spearhead the work of the gospel. They demonstrate God's presence by their actions, establish new Christian communities, and create opportunities for believers to minister.

- *Prophets* are leaders who pass on only what God is thinking and do not taint the message with their own opinions and cultural values. They encourage believers by explaining what God is saying and doing, and by challenging the standards and behaviour of the world and the church.

- *Evangelists* preach the gospel themselves and enable ordinary believers to live the dedicated life of God and gossip the Good News in language which the people around them understand. They help the saints to reach out in witness, they don't do it all for them!

- *Pastors and teachers* build on the foundations laid by the other three leaders. They often stay in one place, perhaps for many years, caring for the church, teaching it the word of God and the ways of Jesus, and helping the people to minister and develop God's kingdom in their locality.

3.   He works with us

We should never stop reminding ourselves and each other of the truth that we are never alone. Jesus is with us by the Spirit.

Matthew 28:20 ☐

Mark 16:20 ☐

He promised to be with us in Matthew 28:20; and Mark 16:20 points out that the promise has been kept. This is the most basic principle of Christian ministry. We are the legs and mouth of Jesus in the world today. We go and speak – when and where he leads – by the Spirit. He confirms our words by special signs. We do not have to worry about miracles, we cannot perform miracles. But Jesus, by the Spirit, works with us and confirms our words – when they are *his* words!

4.   He works through the church

Ephesians
       2:15–16 ☐

In Ephesians 2:15–16, Paul shows that, through Jesus' death, God created one single New Man, and that we all have been reconciled to God 'in one Body'. This means that, though we do all have a personal relationship with God, we are also united with each other.

John 17:20–26 ☐

Jesus' ministry on earth continues through both individual believers and also through the united body – the New Man – the church. Jesus' John 17:20–26 prayer shows how vital our united relationships are in enabling the world to know that the Father sent him.

The New Testament uses a variety of word pictures to describe the united church. Each picture provides us with an insight into an aspect of Jesus' continuing ministry on earth through the church.

Peter's descriptions in 1 Peter 2:9 express similar ideas to Paul's four terms for united disciples – a bride, 2 Corinthians 11:2; a holy temple, 1 Corinthians 3:16; a body, Ephesians 1:23; and the church, 1 Corinthians 1:2.

1 Peter 2:9 ☐

2 Corinthians 11:2 ☐

1 Corinthians 3:16 ☐

Ephesians 1:23 ☐

1 Corinthians 1:2 ☐

- We have been carefully chosen to be *the bride of Jesus*. This means that we are loved with an eternal love and will share Jesus' inheritance of all things.

- We are *the royal priesthood* who serve the king by sacrificially serving the king's people in all sorts of ways, and by filling ourselves – the holy temple or dwelling place of God – with the priestly sacrifices of prayer and thanksgiving.

- We form *the body of Christ* so that he can carry on living his perfect life on earth through us. We are one holy nation, and have been set apart for a corporate life of dedication and consecration.

- We belong to God. We are *his church* (the Greek word *ekklesia* means gathering), citizens of his heaven and children of his kingdom. We are subject to his laws and directed by his Spirit. We do his bidding and establish his kingdom in his way.

We have seen that Jesus' life was shot through with the Spirit. He was born of the Spirit, he lived in the Spirit, and he ministered in complete dependence on the Spirit. Then he baptised the church in the same Holy Spirit so that we can go on living with his purity, serving with his power and revealing the wonderful presence of God.

PART FOUR

receiving the spirit

We have seen that anyone who turns to the gospels to learn about Jesus is faced with John's announcement that Jesus 'will baptise you with Holy Spirit and fire'. Whichever gospel we read, this is one of the first facts we learn about Jesus.

John's announcement at Jesus' anointing is the only event, other than the cross and resurrection, which is recorded in all four Gospels. (Even so, different aspects of the passion are mentioned and emphasised in each gospel, whereas the details of John's announcement are largely the same in all four gospels.)

John's announcement is the only summary of the purpose of Jesus' ministry which appears in all four Gospels. And the placing of John's announcement at the beginning of every Gospel – and its repetition at the start of Acts – seems to be the clearest way possible of emphasising the central importance of 'baptism in the Holy Spirit' in our understanding of Jesus' ministry and of his intentions for all believers.

It appears reasonable to say that, as far as John the Baptist seems to have been concerned, as far as the writers' of the Gospels were concerned, and as far as the Holy Spirit – the inspirer of the writers – is concerned, one of the most important aspects of Jesus' ministry – if not the most important – was that he would be 'the Baptiser'.

We have seen that John's announcement was not an ecstatic prophetic remark which was incomprehensible to the people of his day. On the contrary, his use of the phrase *Holy Spirit* pointed them directly to Psalm 51 and Isaiah 63.

Psalm 51 ☐

Isaiah 63 ☐

It is vital we appreciate that the setting for John's announcement of Jesus as the *baptiser with Holy Spirit and fire* is exactly the same setting as Psalm 51; and that is repentance.

John drew a clear parallel between his baptising in water and the Stronger One's baptising in Holy Spirit and fire. The Holy Spirit and fire were to be the elements of baptism in exactly the same manner as the waters of the River Jordan. Just as John's candidates were immersed in and saturated by water, so Jesus' candidates would be immersed/saturated/overwhelmed/dipped in Holy Spirit and fire.

John's candidates wanted a transformation from the conditions, behaviour and destiny of the unrighteous to that of the righteous. His baptism was both of and for *metanoia* – this is a complete change of mind and attitude to God which results in changed behaviour.

For John's candidates, their baptism was the expression and pledge of their *metanoia* – of their repentance. But it was not just a symbolic gesture – they also expected God to meet them in the River, to accept and facilitate their turning to him, to pledge his forgiveness, and to grant them entry into his kingdom.

John's parallel of his and Jesus' baptism must mean that he expected the attributes of his baptism to be present in the Stronger One's – but with a greater depth, scope, effectiveness and lasting transformation.

John's direct reference to Psalm 51 shows that Jesus' baptism with Holy Spirit and fire would have reference to repentance, and that a consequence of the baptism would be joy-filled service which results in sinners being converted.

Verses 1–17 suggest that having the Holy Spirit relates to:

- *repentance* – verses 1–5

- *knowing the truth* – verse 6

- *purification* – verse 7

- *purity* – verse 10

- *the presence of God* – verse 11

- *effective, powerful, spoken service* – verse 13

- *conversions* – verse 13

- *praise* – verses 12, 14, 15

And John's direct reference to Isaiah 63 showed that Jesus' baptism with Holy Spirit and fire would involve:

Isaiah 63 ☐

- *the presence of God* – verse 9

- *salvation and redemption* – verses 8–9, 16

- *guiding and directing* – verses 12–14

- *powerful signs and miracles* – verse 12

- *glorifying the name of God* – verse 14

The wider use of Spirit that we have seen in the Old Testament is most significant. All John's listeners knew that the Spirit into whom the Stronger One would baptise was the 'breath' without which men and women are dead, the 'hurricane' they could not control or predict, the 'invading force' who brings miraculous results. Genesis 8:1; Exodus 14:21; Judges 3:9–10; 6:34; 14:6; Ezekiel 2:2–3; 3:12; 37:1 all illustrate this.

Genesis 8:1 ☐

Exodus 14:21 ☐

Judges 3:9–10 ☐

6:34 ☐

14:6 ☐

Ezekiel 2:2–3 ☐

3:12 ☐

37:1 ☐

John's listeners knew that the Spirit was a communicator. No Jewish prophet could utter God's words unless he had been prompted by God – Numbers 11:29; Samuel 19:18–24; Joel 2:28; Amos 3:8; Micah 3:8, Zechariah 1:1, 7.

Numbers 11:29 ☐

Samuel 19:18–24 ☐

Joel 2:28 ☐

Amos 3:8 ☐

Micah 3:8 ☐

Zechariah 1:1, 7 ☐

John's listeners knew that the Spirit was given to those who were God's servants – to aid them in their particular calling. The prophets were known as 'servants' and were the main recipients of the Spirit.

They knew that the Spirit was given to the kings to help them rule. They had a hope that, one day, God would raise up another David and would also anoint him with the Spirit. This hope found articulation in the prophecy of Isaiah 11:1–3, perhaps the clearest description of the character of the Spirit in the Old Testament.

Isaiah 11:1–3 ☐

They knew that only a special few received the Spirit. In Numbers 11:29, Moses' reply to Joshua expressed a yearning for a general outpouring of the Spirit. This had been promised in Joel 2:28–32.

Joel 2:28–32 ☐

Every Jew of John's day lived not just in the expectation of the coming Messiah, but also in the hope of the outpouring of God's Spirit. John announced the arrival of both promises: 'Here is the *Messiah* – the Anointed One' and 'He will pour out the Holy Spirit'.

John the Baptist also links the Spirit with fire. As we have seen, this would not have been strange to anyone with an Old Testament understanding of the Spirit. We know that, in the Old Testament, fire was a purifying element more effective and refining than water – and that it was symbol both of God's supreme intervention in history and of his Spirit coming to purify God's children's lives to prepare them for service.

Isaiah 1:25 □
6:5–10 □
Daniel 7:10 □
Zechariah 13:9 □
Malachi 3:2–3 □
Isaiah 4:2–6 □
Ezekiel 36:25–28 □

Isaiah 1:25; 6:5–10; Daniel 7:10; Zechariah 13:9 and Malachi 3:2–3 all show this link with fire. The promise of the Spirit in Joel 2:28 is followed by a description of the dawning of the day of the Lord as 'blood and fire and columns of smoke'. But Isaiah 4:2–6 is the best example: verses 3–4 are an extraordinary parallel to John's announcement.

These Old Testament pictures – which are implicit in John's announcement – show that a baptism in fire is a baptism in the Spirit. In fact, a *baptism in the Spirit* – of necessity – involves wind, water, oil, breath, dove-like characteristics and fire. Ezekiel 36:25–28 is a passage which seems to 'foreshadow' much of what John says and helps us to grasp much of what is behind this important phrase.

Many believers today think about baptism in the Spirit only in terms of what happened at Pentecost. They base their thinking about receiving the Spirit – and measure their experience of the Spirit – around the events of that day.

But Pentecost fulfilled John's announcement of Jesus as *the Baptiser with Holy Spirit and fire* – and this can only be fully understood with an accurate understanding of the Old Testament background.

The New Testament contains five phrases which all describe an encounter with the Holy Spirit. Each of these phrases sheds some light on a different aspect of this experience. We need to appreciate them all if we are to understand what Jesus seeks to accomplish by his gracious gift.

BAPTISED IN THE HOLY SPIRIT

The disciples were people who had been with Jesus throughout his ministry and had been sent out by Jesus in ministry. They had preached. They had seen God work wonderful miracles through them. Yet Jesus told them, in Acts 1:1–11, that they had to wait for 'the promise of the Father'.

Acts 1:1–11 ☐

Jesus promised that – if they waited in Jerusalem – they would soon be baptised in the Holy Spirit. Furthermore, he promised that they would receive power when the Holy Spirit came upon them, and that then they would be witnesses. Their years with Jesus were not enough. Their ministry experience was inadequate. Before they could be witnesses, they needed Jesus to baptise them in Holy Spirit.

This phrase occurs seven times in most English versions of the New Testament. Six of these – Matthew 3:11; Mark 1:8; Luke 3:16; John 1:33; Acts 1:5 & Acts 11:16 – clearly refer to the baptism which John promised that the *Messiah* – the Anointed One – would bring.

Matthew 3:11 ☐

Mark 1:8 ☐

Luke 3:16 ☐

John 1:33 ☐

Acts 1:5 ☐

11:16 ☐

The seventh verse – 1 Corinthians 12:13 – could be translated either as 'baptised by the Spirit' or 'baptised in the Spirit'. However, the phrase 'drinking one Spirit' does suggest that this verse refers to the same baptism 'in' the Spirit as the other six verses.

1 Corinthians
12:13 ☐

The word *baptised* always appears as a verb and never as the noun 'baptism' – which seems to stress the importance of action. It points to an unrepeatable experience of initiation. Baptism – like birth, marriage and death – is something which should occur only once. And it is initiatory in that baptism is not an end in itself – it is not an experience to be enjoyed and then remembered – rather it is the doorway to a new way of living: baptism is essentially the start of something entirely new.

This means that, when Jesus baptised the disciples in the Spirit at Pentecost, it was the unrepeatable moment of initiation into the Holy Spirit's new age. The use of the word 'baptised' shows that nothing would ever be the same again.

But we have seen that Pentecost was also a day of first fruits. It looked forward to a far greater harvest. Each succeeding Christian can enter into the benefits of Pentecost. By faith, we can join them in the baptistery of the Spirit to receive this baptism from the hands of Jesus.

FILLED WITH THE HOLY SPIRIT

We have seen that this expression is foreshadowed in the Old Testament, in Exodus 31:3 & 35:31, where Bezaleel is described as being 'filled with the Spirit of God'. The same expression is then used twelve times in the New Testament to describe one way that people experienced the Spirit – Luke 1:15; 1:41; 1:67; 4:1; Acts 2:4; 4:8; 6:5; 7:55; 9:17; 11:23; 13:52 & Ephesians 5:18.

We should note that Luke (the author of Luke and Acts) uses the phrase to describe what happened to people *before*, *at* and *after* Pentecost. This shows that the believer's experience of the Spirit after Pentecost was similar to the disciple's experience at Pentecost, and to the experience of Jesus and others before Pentecost.

This could suggest that Pentecost was not special. So we also need to note that the word 'baptised' is used to describe only what happened to the disciples at Pentecost. New things began on that day – the widespread availability of the Spirit to all flesh, and the gift of tongues.

Luke uses the phrase to describe the process of becoming filled – Luke 1:41; 1:67; Acts 2:4; 9:17 – as well as the ongoing state of being filled – Luke 4:1; Acts 4:8; 6:5; 7:55; 11:23; 13:52. This shows that the phrase 'being filled' – like baptism – does not point only to an initial experience but also to a new way of living.

Acts 4:31 suggests that, unlike baptism, 'being filled' can be a repeatable experience. The same disciples were filled once in Acts 2:4 and then again, a second time, in Acts 4:31. This does not mean that 'baptism' and 'filling' are two different realities. Every experience of the Spirit is a 'filling', but only the initial one is a 'baptism'.

We have already seen that Luke's use of the Greek verb *pletho* for 'fill' suggests we are not 'cups' who contain the Spirit, but 'sponges' who are filled by being plunged into Spirit. This should help us to understand that being filled and being baptised are similar images.

However, we need to remember that there can be clean sponges and dirty sponges; some are very absorbent whilst others have hard, dry patches – and all sponges benefit from the occasional wringing out and fresh plunging!

Many people know that Ephesians 5:18 is best translated as 'go on being filled with Spirit'. This does not mean repeatedly just asking God to top us up like a half-empty cup! As well as this, it also means opening ourselves up more and more to the Spirit. It means going on asking God to cleanse us so that we become more absorbent to the Spirit. It means begging God to deal with our hard, dry areas so that more of us is saturated by the Spirit.

Ephesians 5:18 ☐

Too many people think about the Spirit in terms of him being 'in us' whereas the New Testament speaks about us being 'in him'. There is a vital distinction between the two. Those who think that they can somehow contain Spirit are implicitly suggesting that they are large enough to control the infinite Spirit – this is an unhelpful individualistic approach.

It is better, and biblically more accurate, to realise that the Spirit is far bigger than us and that we are called to be in him together with all other believers. We can appreciate this corporate approach when we note that individuals are generally recorded as being filled before Pentecost, but groups are usually described being filled after Pentecost.

ANOINTED WITH THE SPIRIT

Like baptism, 'anointing' is a word which is best used to describe a new beginning. It shows that our experience of the Spirit should launch us into something fresh – a new depth of service or dimension of living that we have not known before.

We have seen that prophets, priests and kings were each anointed with oil in the Old Testament only once – right at the start of their ministries – as an act of consecration to God. And we know that Jesus claimed to be the *Christos* – the Anointed – in Luke 4:18–21.

Luke 4:18–21 ☐

And, like baptism and filling, anointing also describes being saturated and surrounded by the Spirit. Perhaps 'showering' is the nearest modern picture to the sort of anointing described in Psalm 133.

Psalm 133 ☐

When we are anointed with the Spirit by Jesus, it means that the Spirit comes upon us and over us: we can say that we are in the Spirit as we would say that we are in the shower. And we will carry on being anointed all the time that we go on living in the shower of the Spirit.

2 Corinthians 1:21 □

1 John 2:20, 27 □

Acts 10:44 □

11:15 □

1 Peter 4:14 □

Matthew 3:16 □

Acts 2:17–18 □

2 Corinthians 1:21 and 1 John 2:20 & 27 describe Christians as people who have been anointed by Jesus with the Holy Spirit. This phrase suggests a once-for-all experience of consecration to God and dedication for service.

The concept of anointing is implied in passages which speak of the Spirit falling – Acts 10:44; 11:15; resting upon – 1 Peter 4:14; coming down upon – Matthew 3:16; and being poured out – Acts 2:17–18.

SEALED WITH THE SPIRIT

2 Corinthians 1:22 □

Ephesians 1:13 □

4:30 □

This expression is used in 2 Corinthians 1:22; Ephesians 1:13 & 4:30. Some leaders argue that this sealing denotes ownership and automatically takes place at the moment of regeneration. But a straightforward reading of these passages indicates both that the sealing is a later event and – as with anointing, baptism and filling – is an action which is performed by Jesus.

This is especially clear in 2 Corinthians 1:22, where the seal is stamped by Christ and is related to the assurance of something which is already in existence.

The normal legal meaning of a seal is plain. It is added *after* the signature as a guarantee of authenticity. When we become Christians, the legal documentation of eternal life is given by the Spirit. God's signature can be seen. But the good news can seem to be too good to believe. Many people lack assurance and wonder if they are mistaken. Then the seal of the Spirit is stamped upon us. It is placed upon us by Jesus to provide authentic, believable, experiential proof of our inheritance.

John 6:26–27 □

John 6:26–27 shows that Jesus is one upon whom the seal has been placed. This must refer to the gift of the Spirit at his baptism – there is not other adequate explanation. So too the coming down of the Spirit at Pentecost was like a seal. It assured the believers that Jesus' promises were genuine.

Although the seal picture does not expand our understanding of the idea of being 'in the Spirit', it does underline the concept of an experience which begins a lasting change, for sealing is both an action and a permanent condition.

RECEIVING THE SPIRIT

This phrase is used twice, in Acts 8:14–17 and Acts 19:2–7. Some people argue that we receive the Spirit automatically when we become a Christian – when we believe in Jesus. Both these passages show that this idea is not credible.

Acts 8:14–17 ☐
19:2–7 ☐

The Samaritans and Ephesians in the stories are clearly identified as 'believers'. They were people who were already Christians. But they had not received Spirit in the way that the New Testament expected.

Some people have suggested a variety of notions to explain away the distance between regeneration and the receiving of the Spirit in these stories. Others have argued that these two stories were included in the New Testament only because they were exceptional.

However, it seems more straightforward to assume they were recorded in the Scriptures because they are thoroughly normal. If they were the exception, why is the normal not mentioned? It is an arrogant theology which suggests that the New Testament is exceptional and that a contemporary experience is normal. Surely the reverse is true.

All these five biblical expressions describe the similar experiences – an initiation into a new dimension, a saturation with a new element, a consecration to a demanding task, a mark of authenticity. It may occur within moments of regeneration, or days, weeks, even years later.

The experience, however described, is always done to the person – we cannot baptise, anoint, fill or seal ourselves. And there is always clear evidence that it has taken place. We know whether or not we have been baptised in water – there will have been witnesses who can confirm it. Baptism, anointing, sealing are visible, tangible provable images. Either we have or we have not received the Spirit. That was the stark question in Acts 19, and there is still no room for uncertainty.

It does not matter much which of the five phrases we use to describe the experience of receiving and living in the Spirit. It does matter that we do receive him, that we go on living 'in' him and that we help and teach others to do the same.

A DISTINCT EXPERIENCE

Conversion – turning to God – is a process which includes repentance, faith in Jesus, forgiveness of sins, baptism in water and receiving the Holy Spirit. The process can be condensed into a few minutes, with all the aspects occurring nearly simultaneously – as for the converts on the Day of Pentecost. Or it can be spread over a lifetime – though, ideally, God does not want it to take that long.

John 3 □

In John 3, Jesus seems to distinguish between seeing the kingdom in verse 3 and entering the kingdom in verse 5. Verse 3 shows that God gives the gift of spiritual sight when people are born again – when they are regenerated by the Spirit. This is when a believer's eternal destiny changes and they start to see things 'God's way' and begin to develop a desire for spiritual matters.

However, verse 5 shows that it is God's will for us not only to be enabled to 'see' his kingdom but also for us to 'enter' deeply into it – to taste it, enjoy it and live in it. It is this entry which creates the possibility (but not the immediate reality) of victory over sin, of power in witness, and of growth into the likeness of Christ.

Whether these are achieved or not depends on an individual's obedience and continued living in the Spirit, but the possibility does not arise without entry into God's kingdom.

John 16:8 □
3:1–8 □
Romans 8:1–14 □
1 Corinthians
2:10–14 □

Regeneration – being born again – is the work of the Holy Spirit. He is the regenerator who is actively involved with the world and unbelievers. John 16:8 shows that he convinces sinners about sin, righteousness and judgement; and John 3:1–8; Romans 8:1–14 & 1 Corinthians 2:10–14 make it plain that it simply is not possible to become a Christian apart from the work of the Holy Spirit.

Nobody can choose to be regenerated, and nobody can make it happen. Nobody knows when it will occur, and people are sometimes unaware or confused when it is taking place. We just know when it has happened for we find ourselves believing what we could never believe before. All this is accomplished *by* the Spirit in the way Jesus describes in John 3:8. It is his work.

John 3:8 ☐

However, it is possible to be regenerated and not to be baptised in the Spirit. This is accomplished *by* Jesus. As we have seen, he is the baptiser; the Holy Spirit is the element.

Here are eight scriptural examples of believers who had been accepted by God but had not been baptised in the Spirit.

1. Most Old Testament saints were believers who were not anointed with the Spirit.

2. The apostles were regenerate, miracle-working believers, but they were not baptised in the Spirit – and did not speak in tongues – until Pentecost.

3. The 3,000 devout Jews of Acts 2 believed in Jesus while Peter spoke. But their receiving of the Spirit depended on their repentance and their baptism in water.

Acts 2:38 ☐

4. The Samaritans of Acts 8 had received God's word and been baptised in water, but they did not receive the Spirit until the apostles laid hands on them.

Acts 8:14–17 ☐

5. Saul, in Acts 9, had recognised Jesus as Lord. Ananias did not need to preach the good news, only to lay hands for healing and the filling with the Spirit.

Acts 9:1–19 ☐

6. Acts 10:4 shows that Cornelius had been accepted by God before Peter arrived and before they received the Spirit.

Acts 10:4 ☐

7. There must have been something about the Ephesian disciples of Acts 19 which caused Paul to ask them whether they had received the Spirit when they became believers. This makes it plain that Paul thought it possible to believe and not receive the Spirit.

Acts 19:1–6 ☐

8. Ephesians 1:13 is another clinching verse which shows that receiving the Holy Spirit is separate and subsequent to belief. The period of time between the two experiences is not important, it is the distinction between them which is critical to understand.

Ephesians 1:13 ☐

Regeneration – being born again – is enacted by the Holy Spirit. This changes our destiny and begins the process of conversion – which includes repentance, faith, baptism and being filled with the Spirit.

Whatever phrase we use to describe the distinct experience of receiving the Spirit we have examined in this section, we can be sure that it has four biblical features:

- *it is initiatory* – it is the beginning of something new – of life in and with the Spirit

- *it is experiential* – something actually happens

- *it is subsequent to regeneration* – it comes some time after we have been regenerated by the Spirit

- *it has vocal evidence* – praise or prophetic speech or tongues is the normal biblical result

Acts 2:42–46 ☐
4:32–35 ☐

Mark 1:12–13 ☐

Romans 8:15–23 ☐

Hebrews 10:15 ☐

Luke 24:48–49 ☐

Acts 1:4–8 ☐
4:31 ☐
6:10 ☐
9:20–22 ☐
10:46 ☐
19:6–10 ☐

There are many biblical evidences of being filled with the Spirit – for example, an increase in spiritual appetite, spiritual attack and assurance. We can see these in Acts 2:42–46; 4:32–35; Mark 1:12–13; Romans 8:15–23 & Hebrews 10:15.

However, Luke 24:48–49; Acts 1:4–8; 4:31; 6:10; 9:20–22; 10:46 & 19:6–10 show that the vocal evidence is the most obvious and immediate. Of course, tongues and prophetic speech are meant to be continuous evidence of an on-going experience – they are not something which should happen once and then stop.

When we receive the Spirit, we start to live in the Spirit and can begin to serve God more powerfully and reveal his presence more clearly – in all the wonderful ways that we are going to study.

PART FIVE

the power of the spirit

Right from the first chapter of the Bible to the last, the Spirit is shown to be making a difference. No matter whether we see him as a hurricane wind or as another person like Jesus, we have to recognise that he is *always* bringing decisive change.

When we study the scriptures, it is easy to concentrate on only one or two of the changes which the Spirit makes. Most sections of the church focus on part of the Spirit's work – and miss out on some aspects of his work.

For example, one group may emphasise his power for witness while another stresses his pure lifestyle, and a third group concentrates on the performance of spiritual gifts and specialist ministries.

If we want to be people who are saturated by the Spirit, who live only in his presence, it is important that we appreciate every facet of his work. We need to be hungry for *every* change that the Spirit wants to make in our individual and corporate lives. We should not try to dictate to him what he should do, or expect him to work in one particular area. We need to be ready for anything!

Luke 1–3 ☐

Matthew 7:28–29 ☐

Mark 1:27 ☐

6:1–3 ☐

Luke 4:22 & 32 ☐

Luke 24:48–49 ☐

Acts 1:4–8 ☐

Acts 4:33 ☐

6:8 ☐

10:38 ☐

In the Old Testament, when the Spirit fell on a select few, he caused them to speak God's thoughts with power, authority and accuracy. It is the same with the New Testament pre-Pentecost fillings. The first three chapters of Luke show how, after their anointings with the Spirit, John, Elizabeth, Simeon, Zechariah, and Jesus all spoke with power and authority.

After (but not before) Jesus' baptism, people constantly remarked upon his powerful and authoritative speech. We can see this in Matthew 7:28–29; Mark 1:27; 6:1–3; Luke 4:22 & 32.

We might think that those disciples who had healed the sick, cast out demons, accompanied Jesus for three years and seen physical proof of his resurrection would be more than adequately equipped to be witnesses. This was not so.

They possessed experience, training and knowledge, but lacked the only acceptable qualification – God's own power, the power of the Holy Spirit. In Luke 24:48–49 and Acts 1:4–8, Jesus promised that the anointing with the Spirit would remedy this deficiency; and we know that the book of Acts is the result.

The three thousand people who were completely converted in one day at Pentecost were the visible fruit and result of the Spirit's power flowing through the disciples. But we know that Pentecost was only the first fruit of the harvest – there was an implicit promise of much more to follow.

As we go through Acts, we can trace how the gospel was first spread by the Spirit's power. For example, Acts 4:33; 6:8 & 10:38 illustrate the centrality of power in the witnessing life of the church.

The most common Greek word for power is *dunamis*: this describes a moral, physical or spiritual ability which resides in a person or object. It is the explosive energy which makes things happen!

Dunamis is the supernatural power of God by which miracles occur, preaching is made effective, and people are strengthened to endure terrible persecutions and adversity.

However, some people who have rightly emphasised the place of the Spirit's power in witnessing have also neglected the place of the Spirit's power in other aspects of the Christian life. The New Testament shows that the Spirit's *dunamis* power for Christian believers has a wide variety of applications. For example, the New Testament shows that God's power enables believers:

- to be a witness to Jesus – Acts 1:8

- to witness to Jesus' resurrection – Acts 4:33

- to do great wonders and signs – Acts 6:8

- to do good and heal – Acts 10:38

- to abound in hope – Romans 15:13

- to perform mighty signs and wonders – Romans 15:18–19

- to speak and preach – 1 Corinthians 2:4–5

- to endure difficulties – 2 Corinthians 6:6–10

- to rejoice in weakness – 2 Corinthians 12:9

- to be strengthened to know God's love – Ephesians 3:16

- to stand against the enemy in prayer – Ephesians 6:10

- to announce the gospel – Philippians 4:13; 1 Thessalonians 1:5

- to be patient – Colossians 1:11

- to share in Christ's sufferings – 2 Timothy 1:7

POWER FOR PUBLIC PROCLAMATION

In the Old Testament, the anointing or filling with the Spirit gave God's servants the prophets the power to receive, understand and speak God's thoughts. By the Spirit, they knew what God wanted them to say and they had God's authority and *dunamis* to say it aloud in public.

In the New Testament, the Holy Spirit enabled *all* believers who were filled with him both to know what to say and to speak it with a power and authority that they did not naturally possess. Paul makes this clear in 1 Corinthians 2:4.

It is important we understand the scriptural emphasise that, at Pentecost, the Spirit transformed the disciples' *public speaking*.

Acts 1:8 ☐

Acts 4:33 ☐

Acts 6:8 ☐

Acts 10:38 ☐

Romans 15:13 ☐

Romans 15:18–19 ☐

1 Corinthians 2:4–5 ☐

2 Corinthians 6:6–10 ☐

2 Corinthians 12:9 ☐

Ephesians 3:16 ☐

Ephesians 6:10 ☐

Philippians 4:13 ☐

1 Thessalonians 1:5 ☐

Colossians 1:11 ☐

2 Timothy 1:7 ☐

1 Corinthians 2:4 ☐

Acts 2:4 shows that when the disciples were filled with the Spirit the Spirit gave them 'utterance'. This is the Greek word *apophthengomai* which is used only here and in Acts 2:14 & 26:25.

Apophthengomai literally means 'to speak forth' and carries the idea of making a public speech – this can be seen in Acts 2:14 & 26:25.

The slightly weaker form *phthengomai* – which means to speak – is used in Acts 4:18. This verse does not contain a total ban on all speaking, but on public speaking about Jesus. If private conversations were banned, *lego* or *laleo* would have been used.

This means that the 'utterance' in Acts 2:4 was a specific Spirit-imparted ability and power to stand up and speak out publicly. It was the 'get-up-and-go' to speak powerfully in public about Jesus – and this was given to all who were filled with the Holy Spirit.

The gift of tongues is a vital feature of Pentecost. It was a distinctive new part of receiving the Spirit – for nobody who had been filled with the Spirit before Pentecost had prayed in tongues. I am sure that we urgently need to rediscover the vital importance of tongues as a sign gift. However, we must equally realise that the Spirit also gave the disciples the power to stand in front of thousands of people and publicly proclaim – in their native language – 'the wonderful works of God' in a way which amazed and attracted their listeners.

POWER FOR MIRACLES

Anointed prophets were those through whom God worked miracles in the Old Testament. Men like Moses, Elijah and Elisha – who had been filled with the Spirit – found not only that God empowered their public speaking, but also that he worked miracles through them.

It is the same in the New Testament. Matthew 21:11, 46; Mark 6:4–15; Luke 7:11–17 & John 7:40 show that the people of Jesus' day constantly assumed that he was a prophet because of the miracles.

The signs and wonders did not make them think that Jesus was divine, rather they understood him to be in the line of Spirit-filled prophets that they knew from their history. The people recognised that the signs and wonders meant God was with Jesus in a special way. This is another key difference that the Spirit makes.

Acts 6:8 shows that the power was the key to Stephen's miracles. And Romans 15:18–19 underlines that the miracle-working power is the power of God's Spirit.

Acts 6:8 ☐

Romans
      15:18–19 ☐

It is important we grasp that the Spirit gives power for miracles essentially in the context of proclaiming the good news about Jesus to those who do not yet believe.

In the New Testament, signs and wonders are mainly given to convince people that the message about Jesus is true. Of course God also heals, provides and delivers because he cares about sick and needy people, but the context is primarily evangelistic.

For example, the book of Acts records:

Acts 3:1–10 ☐
    9:8–19 ☐
    9:32–35 ☐
    9:36–43 ☐

- eight incidents of healing miracles: 3:1–10; 9:8–19; 9:32–35; 9:36–43; 14: 8–10; 14:19–20; 20:7–12; 28:7–10

    14: 8–10 ☐
    14:19–20 ☐
    20:7–12 ☐
    28:7–10 ☐
    2:43 ☐

- six general statements about healing; 2:43; 5:12–16; 6:8; 8:4–8; 14:3; 19:11–12

    5:12–16 ☐
    6:8 ☐
    8:4–8 ☐
    14:3 ☐

- one example of deliverance: 16:16–18

    19:11–12 ☐
    16:16–18 ☐

- three general statements about deliverance: 5:12–16; 8:4–8; 19:11–20

    5:12–16 ☐
    8:4–8 ☐
    19:11–20 ☐

A careful reading of these passages shows that signs and wonders are essentially part of the church's Spirit-inspired and empowered witness to Jesus. This means that power for miracles cannot really be separated from power for public proclamation.

In Acts, miracles had a key role in evangelism and church growth. For example:

- After the lame man was healed, Peter and John were imprisoned and reprimanded, but many of those who had heard Peter's explanation of the miracle became believers.

- The consequence of Saul's healing was his Damascus preaching which led on into his fruitful future.

- When Aeneas was healed 'everybody who lived in Lydda and Sharon saw him, and they were all converted to the Lord'.

- The whole of Joppa heard about Tabitha's resuscitation, 'and many believed in the Lord'.

In Acts, church growth is attributed:

- *fourteen times* – to the association between miracles and the proclamation of the gospel

- *six times* – to miracles alone

- *one time* – to preaching alone (at Corinth)

This should be enough to suggest that a right and natural context of healing is alongside the proclamation of the good news to those who, as yet, do not belong to Christ. Certainly Paul thought so in Romans 15:18–19.

Romans
15:18–19 □

Very few of the people who were healed in the New Testament were followers of Christ. Paul, Lazarus and Tabitha were disciples; and, perhaps, so too were Aeneas, Eutychus and Peter's wife's mother.

However, the other thirty-two people whom the New Testament records as being miraculously healed by the power of the Spirit do not appear to have been followers of Christ at their healing. This must mean that evangelism is the chief context in which the Spirit chooses to work with powerful miracles.

POWER FOR WARFARE

Ephesians
6:10–20 □
1 Peter 5:8 □

Ephesians 6:10–20 and 1 Peter 5:8 show that all Christians are involved in a struggle with the forces of darkness. We may feel weak and inadequate when we think about all the evil in the world, or when we struggle with some regular personal temptation, or when we try to answer people's objections to our faith.

2 Corinthians
10:4–6 □

But passages like 2 Corinthians 10:4–6 promise that the Spirit gives us all the power we need for this sort of spiritual warfare.

The Spirit does not just give us power to speak publicly for Jesus, he also gives us the power to live purely for Jesus. He provides us with the ability to do what we know we ought to do, and sincerely want to do, yet for which we feel we lack the strength.

He gives us the power to say 'no' to cravings for whatever 'the world, the flesh and the devil' seem to be offering – whether obvious vices like addictions to smoking and drinking, or for less obvious vices like ambition, reputation and adulation. He gives us the strength to be patient with people who try our patience, to keep our tempers, to stand firm under pressure, to love the unlovable – in fact, to do all the godly things that the enemy constantly tries to ensure that we do not do.

Of course, some Christians see every difficulty as demonic activity, and are over-concerned with wrestling with Satan. Yet many of the problems we face are just part and parcel of fallen humanity.

The ordinary problems of life can seem overwhelming, but God does give us the grace and *dunamis* we need to overcome our weaknesses and troubles. 2 Corinthians 12:9–10 is a remarkable passage which helps us both to put our own problems into a healthy perspective, and also to think about them biblically.

2 Corinthians 12:9–10 ☐

Time and again, we all have to cry to God, begging him to help us, to strengthen us, to give us power to speak and act in the right way, to make us equal to the pressures we face. And we can be sure that the Spirit's power will be all we need to endure and overcome.

Without exception, we all have to go on fighting evil in its many different forms – both within us and around us. It is crucial we understand that only the Spirit's power can give us victory. We will be defeated whenever we rely on our own resources or experience.

Paul's prayer for *dunamis*, in Ephesians 3:16, should be our constant prayer – both for ourselves and for those whom we love and serve. We desperately need the Spirit's explosive power to help us push back the frontiers of evil in society and establish God's kingdom in our locality.

Ephesians 3:16 ☐

POWER FOR HOPE AND PERSEVERANCE

Most Christians know some of God's promises. But we need the Spirit's power to translate these promises into a tangible experience which fills us with joyful hope in the face of bad news. We need to go on praying Paul's Romans 15:13 intercession for each other.

Romans 15:13 ☐

Many believers are influenced by the world's pressure to seek quick solutions to their difficulties rather than to embrace God's power to persevere through hardships.

2 Corinthians
6:3–10 ☐

Colossians 1:11 ☐

2 Corinthians 6:3–10 and Colossians 1:11 help us appreciate Paul's attitude to difficult circumstances. He knew the truth that God gives patience and grace to endure troubles. We need to remember – and to teach – that the gift of God's *dunamis* for endurance is often God's way for overcoming hardships.

It is the power of the humble Spirit which stiffens our resolve to persevere. It is the *Parakletos* – 'the Encourager' – who urges us to keep going in adversity. It is 'the Spirit of truth' who teaches us to recognise that patience produces faith, and to reject worldly thinking and attitudes.

POWER FOR THE CHURCH

Ephesians
1:19–23 ☐

Ephesians 1:19–23 is one of the greatest New Testament descriptions of God's *dunamis* power – and makes it clear that God gives power essentially within the context of the church.

Recently, there has been a tremendous emphasis in western society on the individual. This has affected the church, and many leaders have over-stressed the importance of an individual response to God.

This important truth must be complemented by the New Testament focus on corporate responses, relationships and activities.

In English, unlike in most other languages, the word 'you' can be either singular or plural. Society's stress on the individual has meant that most of us now instinctively interpret the New Testament 'you's as singular. This means that we think 'me' rather than 'us' when we read a biblical 'you'.

The Greek language, however, distinguishes between a singular 'you' and a plural 'you'. And, in the vast majority of instances, the word 'you' in an English New Testament means a plural 'you all' rather than a singular 'you on your own'.

This means that the promises of God are more for 'us together' than they are for 'us apart'. And this is why the pictures of the church describe one united entity – the body, the bride, the temple, and so on – rather than many small separated individualistic units.

Ephesians 1:19–23 is a healthy reminder that God's power is given mainly in a church setting. Matthew 16:18 states that it is the church against which the gates of hell cannot prevail – not individual believers.

Ephesians 1:19–23 ☐

Matthew 16:18 ☐

This surely means that our prayers for God's *dunamis* power should be 'give us' rather than 'give me'!

POWER FOR WITNESS TO JESUS

When we try to understand the overall purpose for which the Spirit gives us his power, we have to come to a verse like Acts 4:33. The Spirit gives us power to proclaim and to persevere, for miracles and warfare, in order that we will become powerful witnesses to the risen Lord Jesus.

Acts 4:33 ☐

Miracles are not only to thrill and encourage *us*. Victory and hope are not only to make *our* lives more comfortable. They are to provide an eloquent and effective testimony for *others*.

Every aspect of the Spirit's power is given to enable us to know Jesus better, and to help us reveal Jesus more clearly to the needy world around us. The real test of true spiritual power is whether or not it brings people into a deep knowledge and understanding of Jesus.

Jesus' stark warning in Matthew 7:15–23 shows us clearly that the ability to cast out demons, to prophesy, to perform miracles is not enough on its own.

Matthew 7:15–23 ☐

When spiritual power does not bring people close to Jesus; when the motive behind a ministry is selfish, or obedience and truth are absent, or the focus is on a 'Man of God'; whenever there is a 'performance' – it is the Simon Magus spirit we read about in Acts 8.

Acts 8 ☐

In that chapter we see the temptation for power divorced from truth, holiness and moral purity. We see the desire for power both as an end in itself and as a means to an end.

Too many believers pray for power for reasons *other* than knowing Jesus better and revealing him more clearly. And too many leaders try to manipulate divine power at their own will, when they should be experiencing the Spirit's power as they obey God's will.

We should not talk about the Spirit's work in human-centred language – as if God's power is something which is made available for *us* to switch on and *use*. We make ourselves available to him, and he uses us; it is never the other way around.

We must reject the idea that God's power works automatically in us, and that we regulate it by the degree of our consecration and faith. He is the breath of God who blows where he wills – and his gusts vary greatly in strength.

We must take care not to offer the Spirit in our evangelistic speaking as a resource whom unbelievers can harness and control once they have committed themselves to Christ. God's power in us does not immediately cancel out our defects of character and make our lives straightforward and comfortable. Our lives are a continuous fight against the pressures and strategies of the world the flesh and the devil.

The truth is that the Spirit does bring breathtaking changes through his *dunamis* power. And he does provide us with the strength and ability to do what we know we ought to do. This empowering from Christ through the Spirit is a glorious truth which we should want to experience more and more.

But he gives us his power only so that we may know *Jesus* better, and only so that we may reveal *him* more clearly. We have seen that every aspect of the Spirit's genuine work glorifies and focuses on Christ. This must mean that we should always speak about the Spirit and his work in Christ-centred language. Anything else is a mockery of his ministry.

The Spirit's power is given to us – but it is given to turn us into better witnesses, into people whose words and lives – whose everyday behaviour and spiritual authority – show that Jesus is alive in heaven.

PART SIX

the purity of the spirit

Although we often talk about 'the Spirit', we know that he is rightly called 'the *Holy* Spirit'. His name – as with all the names of God throughout the Bible – reveals his nature. He is perfectly holy.

What does being holy mean?

We have seen that the Greek word for 'holy' is *hagios*. For many people, the word 'holy' has moral associations. They think that to be holy means to be very good, perfectly well-behaved, even sinless. But *hagios* is essentially a functional word which means 'totally separated/ devoted/consecrated'.

Hagios is used to describe:

- the Father – Luke 1:49; John 17:11; 1 Peter 1:15–16; Revelation 4:8; 6:10

- the Son – Luke 1:35; Acts 3:14; 4:27–30; 1 John 2:20

- the Spirit – 2 Timothy 1:14; Titus 3:5; 2 Peter 1:21; Jude 20

Luke 1:49 ☐

John 17:11 ☐

1 Peter 1:15–16 ☐

Revelation 4:8 ☐

6:10 ☐

Luke 1:35 ☐

Acts 3:14 ☐

4:27–30 ☐

1 John 2:20 ☐

2 Timothy 1:14 ☐

Titus 3:5 ☐

2 Peter 1:21 ☐

Jude 20 ☐

The Triune God is 'holy' in the sense that he is separated from all creation by his infinite nature: he is 'wholly other'. But God is also separated from humanity by his moral perfection; however, in this case, his holiness – his separation – is a consequence of his sinlessness rather than a description of his sinlessness.

The members of the Trinity – the Father, the Son and the Spirit – are 'holy' in the sense that they are totally devoted to each other. Jesus reveals his holiness in his absolute consecration to the Father, and the Spirit reveals his holiness in the way he exists only to bring glory to Jesus. Their absolute commitment to each other is their holiness.

In the New Testament, believers are also called *hagios* in so far as they are devoted to God – this is sometimes translated as 'saints'. There are many Greek words which could have been used, for example, *hieros* – sacred or outwardly associated with God; *semnos* – worthy or honourable; and *hagnos* – pure or free from defilement. But *hagios* – which describes the nature of the Spirit – is the word used.

Hagiasmos – holiness – primarily signifies separation to God. We can see this is 1 Corinthians 1:30; 2 Thessalonians 2:13; 1 Peter 1:2.

But *hagiasmos* also describes the resultant state of being separated – that is, the conduct which is appropriate to those who are totally devoted, consecrated, committed to God. This can be seen in Romans 6:19, 22; 1 Thessalonians 4:3–7; 1 Timothy 2:15 & Hebrews 12:14.

This means that holiness is not something we aspire to or attain; rather it is the state into which God, in his grace, has called us and in which we live.

We have seen that believers who have been filled with the Holy Spirit are called to stay in the baptistery – to stay in the Spirit, to live in the Spirit, to be filled and directed by him. This means that – from the moment of our anointing – we are living in holiness and with holiness in the same way that we live in the Spirit's power and manifest his power.

The second great work of the Spirit is bringing his holiness into our lives and helping us to live in his holiness with the appropriate purity.

Holiness is the abstract state or condition we enter into when we start to live in the Holy Spirit. Whereas purity (like power) is a practical consequence of that state – it is a manifestation of the Spirit which is seen in our conduct.

1 Corinthians
        1:30 ☐

2 Thessalonians
        2:13 ☐

1 Peter 1:2 ☐

Romans 6:19, 22 ☐

1 Thessalonians
        4:3–7 ☐

1 Timothy 2:15 ☐

Hebrews 12:14 ☐

It is by the Spirit, that God cleanses us from sin's defilement and enables us to resist temptation and do his will. Romans 8:9–16 shows that – as we live in the Spirit – we slowly become more like him and are strengthened by him to put to death the deeds of the body. And 2 Corinthians 3:18 shows it is by the Spirit that we are actually being transformed into the likeness of God.

Romans 8:9–16 ☐

2 Corinthians 3:18 ☐

PURITY FROM SIN

Romans 3:9 teaches that unregenerate human beings are under the power of sin, and Romans 7:20–23 shows that sin still exists in those who have been born again.

Romans 3:9 ☐
7:20–23 ☐

Sin is rebellion against God and any form of self-will in thought or deed. Isaiah 61:8; Jeremiah 44:4 and Proverbs 6:16–19 show that God hates sin and that it makes us filthy in his eyes. According to the scriptures, sin is a guilt which needs to be forgiven or removed, a filth which needs to be washed or cleansed, and also a power which needs to be broken.

Isaiah 61:8 ☐

Jeremiah 44:4 ☐

Proverbs 6:16–19 ☐

Nearly every aspect of the Holy Spirit's work is 'foreshadowed' or introduced in the Old Testament. We have seen that the Spirit enabled the prophets to speak God's words with power and authority, and we have noted passages which show him purging God's people from sin. This can be seen, for example, in these verses.

- Isaiah 61:8 shows that God hates sin.

- Isaiah 4:4 looks forward to a time when Israel will be washed and purged 'by the spirit of judgement and by the spirit of burning'.

Isaiah 4:4 ☐

- Zechariah 13:1 prophecies that a day will come when sin and uncleanness will be dealt with by 'a fountain'.

Zechariah 13:1 ☐

- Malachi 3:2 warns that God is like a refiner's fire and that he will purify his children.

Malachi 3:2 ☐

- Ezekiel 36:25–27 promises that God will cleanse from all filthiness and put his Spirit within his children.

Ezekiel 36:25–27 ☐

John 13:10 ☐
15:3 ☐

Acts 22:16 ☐

1 Corinthians
6:11 ☐

2 Corinthians 7:1 ☐

Ephesians 5:3–5 ☐
5:25–27 ☐

2 Timothy
2:20–22 ☐

Hebrews 9:11–14 ☐
10:22 ☐

1 John 1:7–9 ☐
3:3 ☐

Galatians 5:17 ☐

These verses help us to appreciate that our sinful behaviour really does make us dirty before God. It repels him – in the same way that we are repelled by filth which ought not to be present. However, they also point out that God in his grace is also determined to forgive our sinful behaviour – and to end it.

All the Old Testament purity laws and rituals point to God's cleansing work. This is seen even more clearly in the New Testament descriptions of salvation, especially in these passages which describe washing and cleansing: John 13:10; 15:3; Acts 22:16; 1 Corinthians 6:11; 2 Corinthians 7:1; Ephesians 5:3–5, 25–27; 2 Timothy 2:20–22; Hebrews 9:11–14; 10:22; 1 John 1:7–9 & 3:3.

The Spirit is God's agent of purity. He makes us 'born again'. He provides us with the 'new heart' which creates the possibility – which did not previously exist – of living in purity and of obeying God's commandments. He shapes our lives and regenerates us. He enables us to receive the very nature of Christ – and to become more and more like him throughout our earthly lives.

None of this is automatic. When we receive the Spirit we can and may start to live in his power and holiness but we do not become all-powerful or all-perfect in our own right.

Instead we start walking in the Spirit and begin allowing him to remake us in his image. Galatians 5:17 shows that the path to spiritual power and purity from sin is a long and difficult struggle which means on-going tension and incomplete achievement.

THE BELIEVER'S INNER STRUGGLE

We have to recognise – and explain to others – that there are two opposed sets of desires in every Christian. There are those desires which express the 'natural self-willing and rebelling against God' nature of fallen humanity. And there are those desires which express the 'supernatural God-honouring and God loving' nature implanted in us by the Spirit at regeneration.

These opposite desires mean that, although we are 'living in holiness' in the way that we have considered, we are always finding that our 'hearts' are never absolutely pure. Something always holds us back. For example:

- We never think or do anything that is perfectly right – even though our goal is perfect service.

- We are prevented from thinking what we want to think.

- We know that everything we have done could and should have been better.

- We catch ourselves being proud or weak or foolish.

- We see ways in which our motives and actions could have been better.

- We stretch after perfection, and find that it is always just out of reach.

This does not mean that we never achieve any sort of purity from sin. Far from it, the Christian life is constant advance, not total defeat. The Galatians 5:16 injunction to 'walk in the Spirit, and do not gratify the desires of the flesh' recognises the reality of our struggle with sin, shows that walking or living in the Spirit is the way forward, and insists that we can resist the natural fallen-human desires which assault us.

Galatians 5:16 ☐

Furthermore:

- Romans 7:6 teaches that we have been freed from slavery to sin so that – in the new life of the Spirit – we can and may practise love and righteousness.

Romans 7:6 ☐

- Galatians 5:13–14; Romans 6:17–7:6 & 1 Thessalonians 4:1–8 show that we should do what we can do – this expresses the holiness in which we live.

Galatians 5:13–14 ☐

Romans 6:17–7:6 ☐

1 Thessalonians 4:1–8 ☐

- Romans 8:13 teaches that we can and should put to death sin through the Spirit.

Romans 8:13 ☐

- Romans 8:4 & Galatians 5:16–25 state that we can and should walk in the Spirit – in a steady stream of good works and God-like behaviour which manifests the holiness we live in.

Romans 8:4 ☐

Galatians 5:16–25 ☐

When we walk in the Spirit's holiness, the 'Spirit of truth' ensures we keep on discovering the truths that nothing in our lives is as good as it should be, that we have not fought against natural desires as fiercely as we might have done, that an element of self-will taints even the best things we do for God, that some sinful filth discolours our daily living.

All this means that, when we are living 'in the *Holy* Spirit' we have to keep on throwing ourselves on God's grace, mercy and forgiveness, and keep on asking the Spirit to strengthen us to maintain our inner struggle with sin.

Praise God, the Spirit – as part of his devotion to glorifying Jesus – responds to our cries and acts in several ways, slowly working purity and power over sin into the lives of believers.

PURITY THROUGH STRENGTH TO CHANGE

2 Corinthians 7:1 ☐

As 'the Spirit of truth', the Holy Spirit makes us aware of our faults and failings, and draws our attention to the many different ways in which we disappoint God. He highlights our bad habits and urges us to take note of passages like 2 Corinthians 7:1 and to cleanse ourselves from the filthiness of the flesh and the spirit.

Two of the devil's favourite tactics are:

* tempting us to try and do what God alone can do

* tricking us into asking God to do what he has told us to do

It is important, therefore, that we understand there are two strands to the New Testament purity teaching. There is one element of cleansing which God does himself through the Spirit; and there is a second part which he expects us to carry out ourselves – again, through the Spirit.

Romans 8:13–14 ☐

Romans 8:13–14 makes it clear that 'by the Spirit' we are called to 'put to death the deeds of the body'. God will not do this for us. He will not even do it through us. Instead, he enables us to do it ourselves – by the Spirit.

This means that we should always be moving forward in the Spirit, always walking – with him and in him – deeper into God's kingdom, developing godly habits in every area of our lives. Year by year we should become a little more like Christ as we 'serve in the newness of the Spirit' recorded in Romans 7:6.

Romans 6:17–7:6; Galatians 5:13 & 1 Thessalonians 4:1–8 show that purity is God's will for all our lives. But we can only put to death the deeds of the body' because we have received the Spirit; and we can only 'walk according to the Spirit' because he has come alongside us.

Every day, we all feel both the Holy Spirit's desires and our own fleshly desires. The devil makes each believer think that they are the only one facing this struggle, that some Christians do not have any fleshly desires, and that – if they were a 'proper' Christian – they would not have such desires.

These demonic suggestions simply are not true. Every believer in every generation has to struggle hard to follow the Spirit's leading and ignore their own desires.

Some people think that it should get easier as they grow older and more mature in the faith. But – right to the end of our lives – we are always needing to cry to the Spirit to strengthen our resolve to stay on the path of holiness.

PURITY THROUGH TRANSFORMATION

The spiritual struggle is not self-effort. As we have seen, another strand of purity teaching runs through the New Testament. Many verses use a passive construction to testify that we *are* washed, *are* cleansed and *are* sanctified. God, by the Spirit, works in our lives to bring purity, to shape us in his image.

2 Corinthians 3:18 uses a passive form to show that 'we all *are being transformed* into the same image ... by the Spirit'. The image is that of Christ himself. As we walk in the Spirit, we are changed by the Spirit so that progressively we reflect the Lord's glory and are slowly transformed into his image.

Few passages describe this transformation better than Galatians 5:22–24. It is a word-picture of the truly Christ-like character which supernaturally develops in those who stay living in the Spirit.

Romans 7:6 ☐

Romans 6:17–7:6 ☐

Galatians 5:13 ☐

1 Thessalonians
4:1–8 ☐

2 Corinthians
3:18 ☐

Galatians
5:22–24 ☐

The fruit of the Spirit is not a list of different fruit, rather it is the fullest possible description of one fruit – the one nature of Christ. Just as ordinary fruit naturally develops on healthy, mature trees which are living in the right conditions, so this spiritual fruit develops in believers who are living in the right place – in the Holy Spirit.

This is not an instant transformation. It is a slow but persistent change which God brings to the lives of those who stay in the Spirit. God accomplishes this both through the ongoing revelatory work of the Spirit and also through occasional crisis experiences when we encounter the Spirit and experience his freedom.

Galatians 5:16–26 ☐ Galatians 5:16–26 ties together the two strands of purity teaching. Our responsibility, depending on the Spirit's strength, is to resist selfish fleshly desires. God's free gift, in the Spirit, is a change of nature.

The two strands must stand together. Those who focus too much on 'crucifying the flesh' tend to become legalistic – more concerned with detailed principles than the love of Christ.

Whereas those who over-emphasise waiting for the fruit to grow tend to be casual about sin – they can fail fully to appreciate God's repulsion from every form of evil.

PURITY FOR WITNESS

We have seen that the Spirit's main ministry is bringing glory to Jesus. He works to focus the world's attention on him, to convince unbelievers of sin, righteousness and judgement, to draw sinful people into the love and grace of God.

In the same way that the main purpose of the Spirit's power is to convince people of the truth about Jesus, the main reason for his purity is to show people the true nature of Jesus.

We are called to be pure and are given the gift of the Spirit's purity so that unbelievers around us will see Jesus and be drawn to him. Yet, too often today, there is a gap between what Christians say and what we do: the world considers this to be hypocrisy.

Few things cause people to turn more quickly from God than sinful believers – especially those who seem to claim to be better than they really are. And little draws people closer to Jesus than ordinary lives which radiate God's love and reveal Christ's character.

Purity, like power, is for witness. The Spirit does not work purity in us for our sakes, but for Christ's sake – and for the world's sake. Convincing the world of the truth about sin and righteousness is central to the Spirit's ministry. He is 'The Witness' and he calls us to add our witness to his own so that the world will believe in Jesus.

The fruit of holiness must exist in our lives if our evangelism is to be effective. The way that we live is a vital part of the Spirit's ministry of convicting people about sin and convincing them of the truth about Jesus. But our purity – our single-minded devotion to Jesus – must stand alongside the full power of the Spirit.

We cannot choose between power and purity. It is both or neither, not one or the other! Of course, some Christians do seem to focus solely on either power or purity, but there is great danger in doing this. An over-concentration on power can lead to the Simon Magus spirit, whereas too close a focus on purity can lead to the joyless legalism of the Pharisees.

In Matthew 23:23 and Luke 18:9–14, Jesus condemned the Pharisees because their hearts were not right with God. The Pharisees had started out as a group of people who were offended by the paganism and immorality of their culture. They had wanted to return to godly standards of purity and morality. But what began in holiness – in devotion to God – degenerated into legalism and hypocrisy.

Matthew 23:23 ☐

Luke 18:9–14 ☐

They had focused on purity and forgotten the power of God. They concentrated on rules, and did not know the heart of God. They became judgmental and self-righteous.

We must guard against this today. Not only does it displease God, it also – as 2 Timothy 3:5 shows – turns people away. The Holy Spirit seems to be bringing a new wave of purity into the church, and Satan will try to corrupt it with this sort of moralism and legalism.

2 Timothy 3:5 ☐

Somehow we need to maintain a balance between power and purity in our lives and congregations – and the best way to do this is by personally embracing them both as fully as possible – and then teaching others to do likewise.

PART SEVEN

performance and the spirit

We have seen that the Holy Spirit is powerful – he is God's power in action, the holy hurricane we cannot control or predict. We know that, when we are anointed with him and live in him, he releases and manifests his power through us in his way at his time. It is not that we become powerful, rather that we live in the place where power is.

We have also seen that the Spirit is essentially holy – he is devoted to God and totally committed to glorifying Jesus. We know that, when we are filled with him and walk with him, he releases and manifests the fruit of his holiness through us in his way. It is not that we become pure, rather it is that we live in the place where purity is.

This does not mean that we have no responsibilities. Our part is rather like that of a wise farmer. He knows that he cannot control the weather or change the soil. But that does not mean there is nothing he can do. If he wants to raise good crops, he will sow his seed in a place where the soil is fertile and the weather is favourable. Then he will pull up the weeds and deal with the pests, as necessary.

In the same way, we know that we cannot make ourselves powerful, pure or, indeed, anything worthwhile. If we want to glorify God and share his goodness, we will stand and sow our lives in the most favourable place – in the Spirit. And then, we too will make sure that we deal with 'weeds' and 'pests' as they try to choke and weaken us.

Although exactly the same spiritual principle applies in every area of the Spirit's nature and work, some people do not apply the principle to the important area of spiritual gifts. They speak about gifts as though they possess them, use them, direct and control them.

It is always wrong to say that we 'use' spiritual gifts, for God uses us to manifest his gifts. The gifts are not an ability to do something, but the work of the Spirit through us. They are the energy of the Spirit, not the activity of a believer.

Some people suggest that each believer is given a spiritual gift, and that this then becomes his or her special possession. Questionnaires have even been compiled to help people discover 'their' gift.

1 Corinthians 12:7 ☐   However, in 1 Corinthians 12:7, the Greek verb *didomi* – 'to give' – uses a construction (the present continuous tense) which shows that the giving of gifts by the Spirit to each believer is an on-going activity and not a once-for-all action.

Even more importantly, *didomi* is in the passive form which shows that each person receives the continuous giving from a source which is outside of themselves – from the Holy Spirit. This means that whenever a gift is manifested the believers involved have not dug into their own personal resources, but have passed on what they have at that very moment received from the Spirit.

This shows that the use of different gifts follows exactly the same principle as the demonstration of power and the development of purity. Gifts are an expression of the Spirit's nature, and we will know them when we are in the Spirit.

Isaiah 11:2–10 ☐   Isaiah 11:2 is the clearest description of the character of the Spirit in the Old Testament, and it is the expression of this facet of the Spirit's character which is manifested in the gifts recorded in the New Testament.

Isaiah 11:2 lists seven attributes of the Spirit which have their application in 11:3–5 and their consequence in 11:6–10. These attributes are not gifts which are occasionally given, they are the very essence of the Spirit's being, which will naturally shape and flow out from those who live in him.

We do not have to sweat, pray or wait for these attributes. If we have received the Spirit we will demonstrate them quite naturally.

He is the Spirit of

1. **the Lord** – of *Yahweh*. This shows what we know, that the Spirit is divine. All the attributes which follow are aspects of the divine nature. If we are living in the Spirit, everything we receive comes from the Lord.

2. **wisdom or skill** – of *chakmah*. This is the wisdom which comes from God in Exodus 28:3; 36:1; Deuteronomy 34:9; 1 Kings 4:29; Proverbs 2:6; 3:19; 7:4; 8:1–9:12. Wisdom is not the knowledge of facts, it is the skill to apply those facts in the best possible way.

3. **understanding or intelligence** – of *binah*. This is linked to wisdom in Exodus 35:31; 36:1; 1 Kings 4:29; 7:14 & Ezekiel 28:4. He is an intelligent Spirit, and we do well to rely on his understanding rather than on our own.

4. **counsel or advice** – of *'etsah*. This is guidance or direction. We call it prompting today. We see it in Psalm 73:24; Proverbs 8:14; 19:20–21; Isaiah 5:19; Jeremiah 32:19; 50:45. He is the Spirit who advises us what to say, how to speak, when to act, and so on.

5. **might or authority** – of *geburah*. This is the authority of God which is behind all the words and works of the Spirit. If we speak his words in his way, they will have his authority. Words which we deliver in fear, trembling and holy hesitation are then received as blinding light or scorching heat: they penetrate deeply with permanent effect. People constantly remarked about Jesus' authority, 'not like the scribes and the Pharisees'. This was due to his anointing with the Spirit of *geburah*.

6. **knowledge of facts** – of *da'ath*. The Spirit is not just wise and intelligent. He does not merely give good advice. The Spirit is the all-knowing God. He knows all facts. He knows everything.

7. **the fear or reverence of the Lord** – of *yirah* of *Yahweh*. Although the Spirit is God, his is also one member of the Godhead. As such, he reverences Yahweh. Everything that he does is designed to bring reverence to Yahweh. Every expression of his attributes comes from God and is purposed to increase reverence of God. This principle runs through Scripture.

Exodus 28:3 ☐
36:1 ☐
Deuteronomy 34:9 ☐
1 Kings 4:29 ☐
Proverbs 2:6 ☐
3:19 ☐
7:4 ☐
8:1–9:12 ☐
Exodus 35:31 ☐
36:1 ☐
1 Kings 4:29 ☐
7:14 ☐
Ezekiel 28:4 ☐
Psalm 73:24 ☐
Proverbs 8:14 ☐
19:20–21 ☐
Isaiah 5:19 ☐
Jeremiah 32:19 ☐
50:45 ☐

If we have been anointed with the Spirit and are living in the Spirit, we should expect these Old Testament attributes to be manifested in, around and through us. They should not be surrounded by such a glow that it causes us to believe they can only rarely be experienced.

THE PERFORMANCE OF SPIRITUAL GIFTS

1 Corinthians
12:1–10 ☐

1 Corinthians 12:1–10 is the most well-known passage about gifts – the Greek word *charisma* means 'gift of grace'. Yet some people concentrate so much on the nine gifts listed in verses 8–10 that they miss the wider truths taught in the passage.

The passage shows that:

- there are a variety of *charismata*, but they come from one Spirit
- there are different ministries, but they all come from the one Lord
- there are many activities, but it is the one God at work
- a *charisma* is a manifestation of the Spirit
- *charismata* are given to everyone
- *charismata* are to benefit everyone
- the one and the same Spirit works all the *charismata*
- the Spirit distributes his *charismata* as he wills

1 Corinthians
14:40 ☐

So many Christians have a mistaken attitude to the Holy Spirit that they actively prevent the frequent manifestation of his divine attributes. 1 Corinthians 14:40 can be rendered 'let them happen' or 'let them become', instead of the more common 'let them be done'. We do not create or perform the gifts. We make room for the Spirit to give them.

We are channels for the Spirit's attributes, not a reservoir containing them. We are a sponge in a baptistery of the Spirit, not a teacup to be periodically topped up. We have open access to all the *charismata*, as needed, because we have their source, or rather, because he has us.

1 Corinthians 12:8–10 identifies nine *charismata*. These are not something exterior to the Spirit which he hands on. They are

manifestations of him – they are facets of his character – they are part of his nature, and therefore they direct the church towards Christ.

1. **the word of wisdom** – the supernatural skill to apply a revelation, or to understand how to resolve or assist a situation. We do not gain this through experience or training, but by glimpsing the Spirit's wisdom.

2. **the word of knowledge** – the supernatural revelation of facts about a person or situation. We do not learn this through our natural minds, we see a fragment of the Spirit's knowledge.

3. **healings** – the supernatural knowledge to know whom, how and when God wants to heal a person for the glory of God. This is not an ability we permanently possess, it is something we move in when we walk in partnership with him.

4. **faith** – a supernatural surge of confidence from the Spirit in God's ability to do something seemingly impossible as he chooses.

5. **miracles** – the supernatural operation of miraculous powers through a person, by the Spirit, when God chooses to intervene in the natural order.

6. **prophecy** – the supernatural receiving from the Spirit of a message from God for an individual or group of people.

7. **discernment** – the supernatural insight from the Spirit which identifies the motivating spirit behind a word or person, and which enables the kernel of God's prophetic message to be separated from the human dross which surrounds and accompanies it.

8. **different kinds of tongues** – the Spirit-given words to pray to God in a language which has not been learnt. This frees us to pray with the spirit instead of with the mind.

9. **interpretation or explanation of tongues** – the supernatural revelation from the Spirit of the gist of what someone has prayed in tongues.

These spiritual gifts of God's grace are important for they are tools to help us with the task of glorifying Christ in the world. They are supernatural manifestations of the Spirit which he makes available to all believers who are living in him so that the kingdom of God can be promoted.

But they are *grace-gifts*, not rewards. They do not prove anything except God's essential graciousness and the Spirit's reality and character.

The nine *charismata* listed in 1 Corinthians 12 are examples of the Spirit's manifestations, but they are not an exhaustive list.

- There are other well-known *charismata* in Romans 12:6–8 & Ephesians 4:8–11.

- There are lesser known *charismata* in 1 Corinthians 1:7; 7:7; 13:3; 1 Timothy 4:14; 2 Timothy 1:6 & 1 Peter 4:9–10.

- *Charisma* is used to describe God's work in Romans 5:15–16; 6:23 & 11:29.

- There are obvious gifts – like leading worship – which are not mentioned anywhere in the New Testament.

Many of these gifts are supernatural enhancements of our natural abilities, but the 1 Corinthians 12 gifts are usually entirely new. Either way, through them, the Spirit enables us to do something beautiful and purposeful for God.

He chooses how he will manifest his attributes through each believer. Romans 12:3; Hebrews 2:4 and 1 Corinthians 12:11 illustrate God's absolute sovereignty.

But 1 Corinthians 12:31; 14:1 & 14:12 show that we need to cultivate a desire to be used by God, and a readiness and willingness to build up other people. It is a partnership. We need to 'sow our lives' in the right place – in him – and to weed and remove pests when necessary; but we also need to depend on his warmth and water and power at all times.

Spiritual gifts are not the totality of the Spirit's work. Performance is not the essence of life in the Spirit. Vast numbers of gifts in a person or congregation do not mean spiritual maturity or fruitfulness. Matthew 7:21–23 shows that they neither prove we are pleasing God nor guarantee our salvation.

Paul's first letter to the church in Corinth commends their gifts but rebukes their immaturity, sinfulness and lack of love. It is a distortion of the Spirit's objective for the church when there are gifts without graces, *charismata* without character, spiritual performance without the presence of the Spirit.

Of course the Spirit wants us to make very good use of his gifts – that is why he gives them. But he wants us to manifest them in his way, at his prompting – the focus must be on glorifying Christ and following the Spirit's prompting. We must prefer obedience to performance, and living in the Spirit to performing for the Spirit.

THE PERFORMANCE OF BODY MINISTRIES

Until very recently, the church has assumed that few Christians were equipped for ministry. Full-time male clergy and a tiny number of others were thought to be the only believers whom God wanted to use in helping, teaching and reaching other people.

In part, this was because the Authorised Version of the Bible inaccurately slipped a comma in after 'saints' in Ephesians 4:12 – thus making it appear the precise reverse of Paul's intention.

Ephesians
4:11–12 □

In recent years, however, the Spirit of truth has used more accurate Bible translations to restore the true meaning of Ephesians 4:11–12 to the church – that every member in the body of Christ has a vital ministry role, and that the primary function of church leaders is to equip the saints for the work of ministry rather than to do it for them.

But the devil has tried to ruin this work of the Spirit by tempting some Christians to over-emphasise this truth and make the performance of ministry the focus of their teaching about the Spirit.

We need to recognise that every congregation needs a leader, and that some people have been called and equipped to preach and teach, without ignoring the truth that the leaders and preachers should be motivating, training and releasing the saints in ministry.

And we need to emphasise that the Spirit often gives believers gifts which bear no resemblance and have no relevance to their pre-conversion capabilities. But we must also maintain that many gifts – like teaching – are often ordinary abilities enhanced by the Spirit.

The Spirit has a role for everyone. He wants us all to take part in ministry. He longs for us all to pass on God's words and love to others. But the heart of his ministry is revealing Jesus, making him better known, bringing glory to God, filling our lives with his purity and power.

Spiritual gifts and body ministry are means to a greater end, not objectives to be attained. They are consequences of the Spirit's work, not the main thrust. He most certainly wants to use these things to reveal Jesus. But he wants us to grasp his heart, to share his objective, not to be side-tracked by an interest in structures and small details.

THE PERFORMANCE OF CHRISTIAN ACTIVITIES

In the last twenty years there has been a fantastic multiplying of Christian activities. Churches have been inspired by the Holy Spirit to reach into their communities in a host of caring ways.

Many works have begun among the elderly and young mothers. Schemes have been launched to help the unemployed, the disabled, the housebound and the homeless. New societies have started. Artistic companies have been pioneered. And many congregations have prayerfully developed their worship into more creative and contemporary patterns.

Most of these ventures have been prompted by the Spirit – he is God's agent for change. Nearly all have begun with the holy aim of revealing Christ's love and power to a broken world.

Yet Satan will try to corrupt and distract the believers who are involved in all these projects. He will tempt us to make them an end in themselves, so that – for example – we are more concerned with performing the activity than with pleasing God.

The problem with any stress on performance – whether gifts, ministries or activities – is that God is always more concerned with the internal than the external, with ethics than activity, with motives than deeds.

Philippians
   2:1–11 ☐

Romans 12:1–3 ☐

What matters is being like Jesus. Passages like Philippians 2:1–11 and Romans 12:1–3 remind us that submission to God and sensitivity to each other are vitally important.

These prayers of Paul's show how he intercedes that we will be filled with knowledge, strength and blameless purity – not that we will be enabled by the Spirit to perform amazing exploits: 2 Corinthians 13:9; Ephesians 1:17–18; 3:14–19; Philippians 1:9–11; Colossians 1:9–11; 1 Thessalonians 3:12–13; 2 Thessalonians 1:11–12; Philemon 6.

It is a terrible temptation to measure the Spirit's work in us by the number of activities we are involved with, and by our skill and success in performing them. Whereas the only acceptable measure is the degree to which we have allowed his fruit to develop.

All genuinely Spirit-inspired activities are humble acts of serving God. That is their only importance, to express his *hagiasmos* – his holiness or devotion. We must never think or suggest that actions which are dramatic or eye-catching, which are public and impressive, are more important than lesser or more private actions.

We are doomed to spiritual disappointment unless we fully grasp that the Spirit is pre-occupied with helping us know Jesus better and make him better known. We must ask ourselves whether we really are in the Spirit if we are pre-occupied with anything else.

2 Corinthians
    13:9 ☐

Ephesians
    1:17–18 ☐
    3:14–19 ☐

Philippians
    1:9–11 ☐

Colossians
    1:9–11 ☐

1 Thessalonians
    3:12–13 ☐

2 Thessalonians
    1:11–12 ☐

Philemon 6 ☐

PART EIGHT

the presence of the spirit

We have seen that, as a result of being anointed, filled, baptised in the Spirit we start to live in the Holy Spirit. Our receiving of the Spirit is not an end in itself but the beginning of a new way of life which is lived in and with the Holy Spirit.

We have also seen that when we remain in the right place – in the baptistery of the Spirit – aspects of his nature and character begin to be revealed through us and we begin to be remoulded into his likeness.

We begin to experience and manifest the power of the Spirit. We start to share his holiness and live with his purity. Various attributes of his character – his wisdom, knowledge, faith, might – are revealed to us as grace-gifts from him.

However, we have also seen that our experience and our manifestation of his power, his holiness and his attributes are not ends in themselves. We do not taste his power to become powerful, his holiness to be pure or his attributes to be gifted. Instead, we know these things because we are in his presence and so that we may know Jesus better and make him better known. Any other thought or understanding is a mockery of the Spirit's nature and ministry.

It is wonderful that the Spirit releases the power of God into our lives. It is glorious that the Spirit transforms us with the purity of God. It is marvellous that we receive aspects of his nature as grace-gifts. But these three experiences are merely tokens or evidences of a far more significant work of the Spirit. When we receive him, and go on living in him and walking with him, he brings the very presence of God into our personal and our corporate lives.

MEDIATING THE DIVINE PRESENCE

To bring or mediate the presence of Christ to the church is the essence, the heart, the core, the centre-point of the Spirit's work. It is the one basic activity to which his works of empowering, purifying and equipping must be related in order to be rightly understood.

The single divine strategy – which unites all other facets of his work – is making known the personal presence of the risen Lord – the Jesus of history and the Jesus of heaven – in the church and individual believers.

When we walk with the Holy Spirit, when we experience the presence of Jesus that the Spirit brings, we will have Jesus' resurrection power, Jesus' holy purity, Jesus' divine nature and gifting.

Since Pentecost, the Spirit has been present with believers, changing them to reveal God more clearly and helping them to change themselves to reveal God more clearly – so that Christ may be better known and praised.

Psalm 139 ☐

Jeremiah
        23:23–24 ☐

Amos 9:2–5 ☐

We know that every aspect of the Spirit's work is foreshadowed in the Old Testament. Passages like Psalm 139; Jeremiah 23:23–24 & Amos 9:2–5 describe God's universal presence – the important fact that he is everywhere so we cannot ever escape from his presence. But there are several examples of God being present with a person to bless them in a special way.

Genesis 39:2 ☐

Exodus 3:12 ☐
        33:14–16 ☐

Deuteronomy
        31:6–8 ☐

Joshua 1:5, 9 ☐

Isaiah 43:2–5 ☐

Genesis 39:2; Exodus 3:12; 33:14–16; Deuteronomy 31:6–8; Joshua 1:5, 9 & Isaiah 43:2–5 are all passages which describe God being *with* particular people – or promising to be with them – in a way which enables them to be bold and strong.

This foreshadowing is fulfilled in Jesus – who is introduced by Matthew 1:23 as the ultimate 'God with us', the *Emmanuel* of Isaiah 7:11–16.

Matthew 1:23 ☐

Isaiah 7:11–16 ☐

After describing Jesus throughout his gospel in terms of power and righteousness, Matthew ends his gospel in 28:20 by returning to the idea of Jesus as *Emmanuel*, as 'God with us'.

Matthew 28:20 ☐

The Scriptures show that Jesus is 'God with us'. His presence is the presence of God. Yet Jesus disappeared soon after making that Matthew 28:20 promise, and has not been present on earth in the flesh since his ascension. So how is that promise fulfilled? How is Jesus 'God with us' today?

His promise to be with us was fulfilled by the coming of the Holy Spirit – the *Parakletos*, the another exactly the same as Jesus. Physically, Jesus is at the right hand of the Father in heaven until the day when he comes again. But, spiritually, he is present on earth in the person of the Holy Spirit.

John 14:23 is an extraordinary promise in which Jesus guarantees a degree of intimacy with the Godhead which had only been experienced before in Eden. Yet this promise was given directly after Jesus had promised not to leave his followers as orphans but to give them *allos Parakletos* – the Helper who would be exactly the same as him.

John 14:23 ☐

In John 14:23, Jesus is teaching about the Holy Spirit. Jesus is saying that the Spirit will bring the very presence of *both* the Father and the Son to believers. In the Spirit, the full Godhead will make its home, its permanent earthly residence, in Jesus' human disciples. This means that when we live in and with the Spirit we live in the presence of both the Father and the Son.

THE PRESENCE OF JESUS

2 Corinthians 3:17–18 makes it plain that Jesus comes to us through the Holy Spirit. The passage does not confuse the Holy Spirit with Jesus, rather it explains that we know the presence of Jesus through a vital living relationship with the Spirit.

2 Corinthians 3:17–18 ☐

Romans 8:9 ☐

Galatians 4:6 ☐

Philippians 1:19 ☐

1 Peter 1:11 ☐

It is the same in passages like Romans 8:9; Galatians 4:6; Philippians 1:19 & 1 Peter 1:11 which equate the indwelling of the Spirit with belonging to Christ.

Everything Jesus says to us or does through us is accomplished by the Spirit – because Jesus is present by the Spirit. The presence of the Spirit is the presence of Christ – and vice versa. This means that we will commit ourselves to developing and maintaining a relationship with the Holy Spirit if we are serious about knowing Jesus better.

The simplest way we can understand the ministry of the Spirit is in terms of mediating Christ's presence to us – all his works and activities are part of this mediation. He gives us such a deep knowledge of Jesus' presence with us that three things keep on happening.

1.   The personal fellowship of his presence

John 16:12–14 ☐

In John 16:12–14, Jesus explains how the Spirit will take the things of Jesus and makes them known to us. He will guide us into Jesus' ways and teach us Jesus' truths. He will not pass on his own thoughts, rather he will communicate what he hears and receives from Jesus.

Jesus' first followers walked and talked with the Lord. They listened to his voice, learnt from his words and actions, felt his love, and lived in close fellowship with him.

This intimate fellowship with Jesus still continues today as we experience his presence through the Holy Spirit. When we listen to the Spirit, we hear the words and voice of Jesus – reminding us of his love and guiding our thoughts and actions. This can be seen in Revelation 2 & 3, where Jesus' personal message is 'what the Spirit says to the churches'.

Revelation 2 & 3 ☐

We do not hear Jesus audibly. Instead, the Spirit speaks to us in a variety of ways:

- through the Scriptures

- through other believers

- through God's creation

- through spiritual gifts

- in our own inner spirit

2. The personal transformation of his presence

To some degree, we are all influenced by the people with whom we spend a great deal of time. It is the same with Jesus. The more time we spend in his presence, in the Spirit, the more we become like him. The longer we listen to his words, the more they control our thoughts – and so on. We can see this in 2 Corinthians 3:18.

2 Corinthians
3:18 ☐

When we saturate ourselves in the four gospels, gazing at Jesus to grasp his attitudes and motives, we can begin to appreciate how we should think and behave. But this can remain an intellectual process, a shaping and moulding of ideas; we do not begin to be transformed until we are actually in the presence of Jesus – until Jesus is in us by the Spirit. Only then can our motives be moulded and our wills be energised.

We have seen that Jesus' ministry had several themes. He called people to obey him as king, to depend on him as saviour, to follow his perfect life, and to worship him as holy God. In the Spirit, Jesus is present both in and with us in all these aspects of his nature and ministry.

- The king of kings, the conqueror of evil, the ruler over sickness, the judge of the whole earth – he is with us. We live in his presence. Nothing we think or do is missed by him. By the Spirit, the king speaks to us.

- The suffering servant of humanity, the shepherd who lays down his life for his sheep, the blood-stained substitute who bore God's wrath against sin – he is with us. By the Spirit, the suffering servant points out his sacrificial way of living and dying.

- The ideal human being, the perfect specimen of humanity, the pattern life for all humankind, the sympathising friend of sinners – he is with us. In the Spirit, we live with him and he lives with us. By the Spirit, the Son of Man shows us that he really does understand our weaknesses – but he still accepts us and urges us to go on following him more closely.

- The glorious light-bearing, life-bringing Son of God, the living Word, the complete revelation of the invisible Father – he is with us in the Spirit. By the Spirit, the living God fellowships with us. This must make a difference to our lives. How can anyone be in the presence of Jesus in this way and remain unchanged?

3. The personal assurance of his presence

Romans 8:16 ☐

Romans 8:16 promises that the Holy Spirit will help us to know that we are children of God, that we heirs of God, and that we are joint-heirs with Christ.

The presence of Jesus in us and with us by the Spirit is all the proof anyone needs that we are loved and accepted by God. The presence of the Spirit is the 'seal' which assures us that we have been forgiven, that we have been redeemed, that we have been reconciled and that we have been welcomed into God's family.

Genesis 8:9–14 ☐

In Genesis 8:9–14, the dove brought Noah assurance that God had not forgotten him. The presence of the dove was the revelation of hope and promise. The descent of the Spirit at Jesus' baptism 'as a dove' was related to the voice which gave Jesus assurance of his Sonship, the Father's love and divine pleasure.

Hebrews 10:14–15 ☐

Hebrews 10:14–15 also makes clear the Spirit's dove-like work of assurance. Our doubts should fade when the Spirit reveals the presence of God to us.

We find that we know because we know. A deep, unbreakable certainty of adoption, an immovable conviction of the Father's love is experienced which makes circumstances seem irrelevant. This is not obstinate arrogance, it is the work of the Holy Spirit.

THE PRESENCE OF GOD

Many people have some sort of belief in a God who is 'out there somewhere'. The evidence of creation and their own fallen nature combine to make them think that some sort of supernatural being must exist. They do not know him. They have some strange ideas about him. But deep down – even if only when faced with a crisis – most people believe in a God who is 'there'.

People of all religions believe in a God who is tangibly real, and they credit him with varying degrees of power and benevolence. Christianity is different. Added to our belief in the living God who is everywhere, who made and sustains all things, we uniquely claim that he is here with us.

We know that Jesus was the perfect revelation of the invisible God, and therefore understand that knowing Jesus means we must also know the Father.

Jesus came to reconcile us with the Father, to 'bridge the gap' between us and God. John 14:23 makes it particularly clear that the Spirit reveals not just the Son to us, but – through the Son – the Father. This shows that the coming of the Spirit means we enjoy not only the presence of Jesus, but also the presence of the Father.

Since Pentecost, the Spirit has been actively revealing the presence of God. At times it may be popular to talk about power and purity, but we need to understand that there can be no more important work than revealing the presence of God in our dark and evil world.

We have seen that the New Testament makes much of the Spirit's power and purity. However, it makes even more of him mediating the presence, the word and the activity of God.

For example, in the New Testament:

- the Spirit is always presented as the Spirit of Jesus Christ, God's Son – Acts 16:7; Romans 8:9; Galatians 4:6; Philippians 1:19 & 1 Peter 1:11

- the Spirit whom we receive is the same Spirit who was with, in and upon Jesus – Luke 3:22; 4:1, 14, 18; 10:21; John 1:32; 3:34; Acts 10:38

- Jesus, the Anointed One, is the Spirit giver – John 1:33; 7:37–39; 15:26; 16:720:22; Acts 2:33; 1 John 2:20, 27

- the coming of the Spirit to the disciples after Jesus had been taken from them was, in a real sense, Jesus' return to them – John 14:16, 18–21

- the indwelling of the Spirit of God, who is the Spirit of Christ, is described as the indwelling of Christ himself – Romans 8:9–11

- the Spirit is the Lord and he is transforming us into the image of the Lord – 2 Corinthians 3:7–18

These passages conclusively show that the Spirit's essential work since Pentecost is mediating the presence, word and activity of God.

John 14:23 ☐

Acts 16:7 ☐
Romans 8:9 ☐
Galatians 4:6 ☐
Philippians 1:19 ☐
1 Peter 1:11 ☐

Luke 3:22 ☐
4:1 ☐
4:14–18 ☐
10:21 ☐

John 1:32 ☐
3:34 ☐

Acts 10:38 ☐

John 1:33 ☐
7:37–39 ☐
15:26 ☐
16:7 ☐
20:22 ☐

Acts 2:33 ☐

1 John 2:20 ☐
2:27 ☐

John 14:16
18–21 ☐

Romans 8:9–11 ☐

2 Corinthians
3:7–18 ☐

It is only by grasping this basic biblical principle that we can have a clear understanding of the Spirit and of much of the Christian life.

THE PRESENCE FOR GLORY

In the Old Testament, the expression 'the glory of God' is used in two ways. It refers both to the self-revealed character of God, and also to a visible revelation of God's presence. This means that God's glory shows people both where God is *and* what he is like. Glory is the outward manifestation of God's absolute holiness.

God's glory:

Exodus 24 ☐

Leviticus 9:6–24 ☐

1 Kings 8:1–11 ☐

- appeared to the seventy elders on Mount Sinai – Exodus 24

- was regularly seen in the wilderness tabernacle at the hour of sacrifice – Leviticus 9:6–24

- filled the Jerusalem Temple 1 Kings 8:1–11

In the New Testament, these aspects of God's glory were perfectly fulfilled in Christ. He is both the complete self-revelation of God's character and also the clearest revelation of God's presence.

The word 'glory' normally describes Jesus' revelation of God's nature by grace and miracles. It adds to the Old Testament the sense of a demonstration of beautiful perfection and a display of magnificent power. God's glory seen in Jesus shows the Father's splendid excellence and the full extent of his authority and power.

Since Pentecost, it has been the church's function to reveal God's great glory in and to the world. This means that we are meant to be showing God's holy character to the world, to be being seen by the world as the place where God lives, and to be demonstrating God's regal authority and power.

It is obvious that we can glorify God only by being full of the presence of God – and that is the work of the Spirit.

When we pray for God's glory to be seen, we are asking for the world to see his holiness, grace and power – and they see that in us through the Spirit's work. As he brings God's presence to us, so God is glorified in the world through us.

HIS PRESENCE FOR WITNESS

Jesus' words about the Holy Spirit in John 14–16 introduce the Spirit's work of bringing glory to Jesus. However 'glory' has become such a 'religious' word – one used mostly in worship – that we sometimes forget the word is mainly about witness.

One way of illustrating this is to think of disciples like the moon. The moon is quite dead by itself, but it shines gloriously in the darkness with the reflected light of the sun. The moon is eclipsed when the earth gets wholly or partly between the sun and the moon. In the same way, there is spiritual darkness in the church when the world gets between the Son of God and believers.

However, the sun is eclipsed when the moon gets between the sun and the earth. And there is a similar spiritual darkness on earth when disciples take the limelight and hinder the passage of light from the Son of God into the world, drawing attention to themselves instead of reflecting his glory.

We can also think of the Spirit like a floodlight. It is a wonderful spectacle to see a magnificent building floodlit at night. The Spirit glorifies God by shining his light on God and focusing all his energy on him. When floodlights are well-positioned they are completely invisible – we can only see the light they radiate and the building they illuminate.

When we are 'in the Spirit', we are rather like a theatrical lighting operator. We receive our instructions from the producer, and are pre-occupied with focusing the spotlights on God. We cannot make the lights happen, we can ruin the spectacle by not following the instructions, yet we have a role in partnership with the lights and the producer. And we are noticed only when we get something wrong!

In John 14–16, all the different strands of the Spirit's work we have examined are present – power, purity, presence, glory are so on. But through all this, an evangelistic heart beats loudly.

John 15:26 ☐

John 15:26 states that the *Parakletos* will be Jesus' witness – and that we will also be his witnesses. It is impossible to separate the work of the Spirit from witness. Everything he does is a witness to Jesus. Every change that he brings to our lives is meant to make us better witnesses to Jesus – to bring him more glory.

The Spirit surrounds and fills us with his power so that people will believe Jesus rose from the dead. He saturates us with his holiness so that our behaviour does not cause people to stumble. And he brings the presence of Jesus to our lives so that, wherever we are, we reveal the glorious nature of God.

The Spirit takes the things of Christ and makes them known to us: and this brings glory to Jesus. He achieves this through a vital, living, personal relationship which he continually seeks to establish with us.

Christ will be glorified in us when we develop and maintain this relationship with the Spirit. We will know Jesus, we will know the Father, we will walk in the ways of God, and – most important of all – we will be accurate and effective glorifying witnesses in the world to the living Lord Jesus.

PART NINE

partnership with the spirit

We have seen that the Bible uses two basic pictures to describe our relationship with the Holy Spirit. Firstly, the Scriptures use words like 'baptism', 'anointing' and 'filling' to show that we are meant be placed in the Spirit by Jesus so that we are saturated by the Spirit. We are then called to go on living 'in the Spirit' so that he can go on glorifying Christ through us.

This image stresses the corporate dimension, for we are all together 'in the Spirit'. By being 'in' the right place, the Spirit's attributes can be manifested through us and can transform us into Christ's likeness.

Secondly, the Scriptures portray our relationship with the Spirit in a way which emphasises the personal dimension. By introducing him as the *Parakletos*, Jesus shows that the Spirit is called alongside us to be 'with' us. This highlights the way we relate to the Spirit as a partner.

Neither picture is adequate on its own to describe the mystery and the richness of our relationship with the Spirit. Somehow, we must embrace both ideas at the same time, and make sure that we communicate both in our speaking and teaching.

2 Corinthians
13:14 □

This means that we are both 'in the Spirit' and 'with the Spirit'. We are overwhelmed, saturated and immersed in the Spirit. But we also walk with him in partnership.

At the end of meetings, Christian people often use 2 Corinthians 13:14 to bless each other. This illustrates that when the Bible speaks about the Son, the main word is 'grace'; that when it describes the Father, its central idea is 'love; and that when it introduces the Spirit, its key word is 'fellowship'.

The Greek word for this is *koinonia* – which means 'sharing together in something purposeful'.

The idea of 'fellowship' has been devalued by its use in some Christian groups. For many believers, it means little more than a polite chat after a service. Yet *koinonia* means sharing closely together in something active and dynamic.

Koinonia is the word for a partnership which has a clear common purpose. Fellowship is active not passive. It is dynamic, not insipid. It involves communication, co-operation, contribution, direction, action and accomplishment. Genuine scriptural *koinonia* partnership or fellowship always has both a goal and an outcome.

It is not enough to say that we know the Father, to insist that we know the Son, and then to ignore the Holy Spirit – for knowing the Spirit is the key to knowing the Father and the Son!

The Spirit is the Spirit of *koinonia*. He is the *Parakletos*. He comes alongside to create a relationship – a partnership with a purpose. Together, the Spirit and I, the Spirit and you – will do our utmost to bring great glory to Jesus in our bruised and broken world.

DEVELOPING THE MINISTRY OF JESUS

God has forged our partnership with the Spirit – our living with the Spirit – so that Jesus' ministry can continue. It is our responsibility to develop this relationship with the Spirit – so that Jesus' ministry can become more effective wherever we are.

Discipleship

Living effectively in partnership 'with' the Spirit depends on discipleship. Jesus' first partners in ministry were called 'disciples'. This means that the degree to which Jesus' ministry develops in us depends on our commitment to discipleship.

We need to follow Christ's example in everything – in our thinking, speaking, living, praying, compassion, serving, ministry and morality.

Discipleship means rejoicing when persecuted, initiating reconciliation, speaking simply, giving generously, loving enemies, living humbly, rejecting materialism, judging nobody. It means feeding the hungry, clothing the naked, visiting the imprisoned, welcoming foreigners, comforting the sick, and so on.

When we live with the Spirit – the same Spirit who was with Jesus – we are bound to hear the Spirit prompting us to think and act like Jesus. We will feel his quiet prompting to do this, to go there, to sit quietly, to be silent, to send a gift, to speak a brief sentence, and so on.

As it is a genuine partnership, the Spirit does not force us obey him. And, as it is a committed relationship, he does not desert us when we act foolishly or sinfully. He is always 'God with us'.

Guidance

The Spirit does not start guiding us when we submit to him. He has been at work, speaking quietly to us, from before our regeneration. Obviously, we draw closer to him when we are baptised in him by Jesus. No matter what we think, we all hear his prompting, but we may not necessarily recognise his voice or submit to it.

We often feel something inside our minds, and are not sure whether it is the Spirit's prompting, our natural aspirations, or devilish confusion. Sometimes we find ourselves suddenly focusing on a particular person; at other times we feel that we should say or do something. But we may not know what to do with these feelings.

If we are living with the Spirit – in his presence – we must expect him to guide and direct us with his gentle, quiet voice. But he does not compel us to obey him. He encourages. He advises. He persists. But he does not insist!

We need to learn to recognise his voice and be able to distinguish it from our own ideas and the devil's suggestions. We can only do this by acting on these inner promptings and being ready to make mistakes and look foolish. There is no other way.

It has been so stressed in the church that prayers should be made to the Father, that many believers find it difficult to develop an intimate relationship with the Spirit. Some think that he can speak to them but they cannot speak to him. But we do not always need to be interceding and wrestling with the Father. Sometimes it is right to pray in a more conversational way with the Spirit. Of course, we cannot intercede to him, as he helps us to intercede. However, we can talk to the Spirit in fellowship and in dependence on his help.

DEPENDING ON THE SPIRIT

There is great pressure in society to appear competent and successful. Yet we only make spiritual progress when we grasp that we can do nothing on our own. We have been made for a relationship with God – which we experience on earth in fellowship with the Spirit. Only by depending fully on the Spirit can we begin to minister in the Spirit.

1 Kings 18 ☐

1 Kings 18 demonstrates the difference between a Spirit-filled true prophet and false-prophets. Elijah did not try to make anything happen. He did not strike a spark and ask the people to believe that this was the fire of God. In fact, he did everything possible to prove to the people that he was not the cause of the miracle.

Instead of putting fire under the sacrifice, he poured gallons of water over it. As far as he was concerned, it had to be God or nothing. By his words and actions, Elijah ensured that nobody could think he had been anything more than God's mouthpiece.

God or nothing

Like Elijah, we need to make it hard for watching people to think that what happens in the church is due to manipulation or pressure. It has to be as clear as possible that it is God or nothing.

We can see this in Jesus' ministry. When we read the gospels we see that he either went directly to specific individuals or responded to particular requests. For example, in John 5, Jesus did not make a general appeal for sick people who wanted healing to identify themselves. Instead, he listened to the Spirit and was led directly to the person with whom God was dealing.

John 5 ☐

No exaggeration

One of the most striking features of Jesus' ministry is the way that he often asked people to tell *nobody* about the miracle. Mark 7:31–37 and 8:22–26 reveal this holy desire to work unobtrusively – which is one of the hallmarks of the humble, self-effacing Spirit.

Mark 7:31–37 ☐
8:22–26 ☐

- Jesus did not use people who had been healed to publicise his ministry.

- He did not press them to testify in an attempt to attract more people to his message.

- He never tried to impress people by exaggerating what had taken place.

We must be careful that we do not make false claims, that we never overstate events, and that we do not use words like 'the best' and 'the greatest' which are rarely true.

If we are serious about depending on the Spirit of truth, we will be characterised by his humble, straightforward speech, and will not feel the need to use worldly methods of self-publicity which overstate facts, ignore mistakes, and focus attention in the wrong direction.

The Spirit's anointing

Depending on the Spirit means relying on our anointing with him by Jesus. This is where developing Christ's ministry and depending on the Spirit draw together – as we have seen, anointing is central to his ministry.

People are sometimes confused by the phrase 'anointing' as it is used to describe a wide variety of spiritual experiences.

As we have seen, there is:

- an *initial anointing* when Jesus baptises us in the Holy Spirit

- a *continual anointing* which describes our state as believers who are living in and with the Spirit

- moments of *special anointing* when God, by the Spirit, equips us in a special way for a particular need, office or aspect of ministry

Once filled with the Spirit, we are *continually anointed* while we go on living in that anointing. However, there will be occasions when God is with us in a special way. Living with the Spirit is unpredictable. He is a hurricane who blows where he wills, not a tame God who does what we expect. When we are in partnership with him, we must expect periods of calm interrupted by moments of extraordinary activity.

Some people seem to forget that anointing equips us to do only what the Spirit directs. We are anointed with the Spirit *himself* not with a particular ability. This means that we must remain in step with him for the anointing to be effective.

Acts 18 ☐

Acts 18 describes two years in Paul's life when he worked in Corinth as a tentmaker, held debates in the synagogues, founded a church, and travelled through Galatia. He was anointed all this time. He was in and with the Spirit. But there are no records of any miracles.

Acts 19:11 ☐

Yet when Paul moved on to Ephesus – where he stayed for another two years – Acts 19:11 comments that 'God worked unusual miracles by the hands of Paul'. Why were there unusual miracles in Ephesus and not in Corinth? Why, when Paul later moved on to Caesarea for two years, are there no records of any miracles there either?

We can either conclude that Paul was not walking in step with the Spirit in Corinth and Caesarea. Or we concede that Paul had a special anointing in Ephesus because unusual miracles were on the Spirit's agenda for the town at that time.

DISCERNING THE SPIRIT'S AGENDA

It is a basic ministry principle that God does not give power for what he is not doing, but always provides power for what he is doing.

Jesus, who was fully God and – as a man – had received the Spirit without measure, appears not to have healed everyone. Instead, the gospels suggest that Jesus healed all who were brought to him, and that he took God's healing to specific individuals – ignoring crowds of other sick people around them. Clearly, he did only what the Father was doing – he stuck rigidly to the Spirit's agenda.

We are doomed to disappointment and embarrassing failure if we try to take the initiative in ministry or follow our own inclination. We must wait for the Holy Spirit and receive specific directions and revelation from him before we proceed in active ministry.

Waiting

Knowing God's will is one of the hardest parts of the Christian life. Our problem is not so much obeying God as knowing what to obey.

We long to obey him. We know that is the best and right thing to do. But we do not always know what he wants us to do. Instead of waiting for direction, we presume and do whatever seems to be best.

John 10:16, 27 are promises which Jesus has kept. By the Spirit, we do hear Christ's voice. Sometimes, however, we are not sure whether it is his voice or our own thoughts or demonic temptations. At other times, our minds are so full of clutter and distractions that we cannot hear his voice clearly. We know that he is speaking to us, but we cannot make out what he is saying.

John 10:16, 27 ☐

We need to wait patiently on God – creating an oasis of peace in our lives through meditating on his word – before we start listening for the Spirit's direction.

Listening

We all need to spend more time in listening prayer than we do. Too often, we spend time asking God to do things rather than asking him what we should do – and listening for his reply.

Asking God specific questions is a good way of learning to identify God's voice. We should not be frightened to ask God what we should do or say. But we must act on the thoughts which come into our mind.

We will learn to recognise God's voice by acting on what we hear in our inner spirit. Some people are so worried about doing something wrong that they never do anything! Whereas others are so confident that every crazy thought is a divine instruction that they say and do ridiculous things. This means that we need to develop discernment when we listen for God's answers to our questions.

With time, we begin to recognise the Spirit's special way of speaking to us. We should never stop spending time alone with him; however, we will increasingly recognise his way of interrupting our natural thoughts when he wants us to speak to someone. Some of the most precious times of ministry occur when we trust these sudden, unsought thoughts.

God is concerned about every aspect of our lives. Too many believers think that 'ministry' means nothing but miracles, so they ignore the 'everyday' thoughts which the Spirit places in our minds. Living in fellowship with the Spirit means being ready to be involved in anything on his agenda – small, unseen words and deeds of comfort, as well as more public signs and wonders.

Asking

When we are ministering to a person, we need to listen both to God and to the person we are helping.

Mark 5:9 ☐

8:23 ☐

9:21 ☐

Luke 18:41 ☐

John 5:6 ☐

As well as functioning supernaturally, Jesus also worked at the natural level of observation and deduction. He asked normal and natural questions which helped in ministry. If he needed to ask the questions in Mark 5:9; 8:23; 9:21; Luke 18:41 & John 5:6, so will we.

As well as asking the person questions, we always need to ask God what else needs to be known. We should ask God to show us what is happening, what caused the problem, what he wants us to do, and so on. This is examined in the *Sword of the Spirit* book, *'Ministry in the Spirit'*. The Spirit may give us a picture or word to pass on, suggest a statement we should make, or put a question into our mind. The cause of the problem is often self-evident, but sometimes we need God to reveal whether it is physical, emotional, spiritual, demonic, hereditary or a curse. If God tells us nothing, we know all we need to know.

We have to depend on the Spirit. We must listen to his instructions. If we catch ourselves saying and doing the same things that we have said and done before, there is a good chance we are depending on experience rather than the Spirit!

Once we have asked all the relevant questions, we do not look in a book for the appropriate solution or action. We turn to our partner, the Holy Spirit, for directions.

DEMONSTRATIONS OF THE SPIRIT

When we partner the Spirit, we share his calling to glorify Jesus and bear witness to him. Sometimes we will be called to minister in a meeting, but we will usually be directed to minister in everyday life.

Most people were ministered to by Jesus when he was on a journey. Others were healed by him in their beds, in a garden, at a funeral, at a meal and so on. It was the same in the early church. People were reached in the street, on the way to a prayer meeting, in private homes, out in the countryside, and at an open-air evangelistic rally.

God seems to delight in ministering at the roadside, in the course of daily living, in helping social outcasts who will never attend a church meeting. We should remember this if we want to share in the 'greater things' promised by Jesus.

When the Spirit prompts us to speak and act – whether in a supermarket or office, a bus or back garden, a private home or even at the dentist – there are five simple principles to remember.

1.   Prayer

Genesis 20:17; 1 Kings 13:6, 17:20–22; 2 Kings 4:33–36; 20:5 & Acts 9:40 show that prayer is a vital part of ministry.

- John 14:12–14 & 16:24 are great promises. We do well to begin ministry by claiming these promises and making brief *petitions* asking God to do what is on the Spirit's agenda.

- Romans 8:26–27 promises that the Spirit helps us by making *intercessions* according to God's will. We are not on our own – we have a partner who is interceding for us. At times, it is right to suspend ministry for a few days so that we can have a prolonged time of intercession before continuing.

Genesis 20:17 ☐

1 Kings 13:6 ☐
     17:20–22 ☐

2 Kings 4:33–36 ☐
     20:5 ☐

Acts 9:40 ☐

John 14:12–14 ☐
     16:24 ☐

Romans 8:26–27 ☐

Acts 3:16 ☐
      9:17, 34 ☐
      14:10 ☐

James 5:15 ☐

Mark 11:24 ☐

- Prayers of *pronouncement or command* feature strongly in the New Testament accounts of ministry – for example, Acts 3:16; 9:17, 34 & 14:10.

- James 5:15 introduces the prayer of *faith* – which is a special impartation of faith given for that moment. We often pray with little expectation of anything happening. Yet, now and again, God overwhelms us with his faith and we pray as Jesus described in Mark 11:24.

2.   Gifts

We have seen that God's giving of grace-gifts to each believer is an on-going activity and not a once-for-all action.

This means that we do not receive gifts as personal possessions, but that we are given whatever attribute of the Spirit's nature we need when we need it.

Jesus used all the gifts of the Spirit in ministry, except tongues and interpretation, and we can expect to do the same. We do not need to worry about defining the gifts, as the New Testament does not do this, rather it encourages us to use them.

In ministry, we need to rely on our partner the Spirit to provide what we need, then we should trust the thoughts he gives and act on them.

Mark 9 ☐

Obviously we will make mistakes. The disciples failed Jesus in Mark 9, and we will fail him too. But we will develop more skill in manifesting the gifts if we persevere through the failures and errors.

3.   Faith

Some believers think that they need huge amounts of faith for ministry, whereas Jesus suggested that we need only a tiny amount – the size of a mustard seed.

Faith is like the clutch in a car. There might be a powerful engine roaring under the bonnet, but the car remains stationery until the driver presses the clutch and slips the gear. The clutch does not make the car move, it merely engages the power.

Matthew 9:2, 22, 29 & Mark 6:1–6 show that we do need some faith in ministry. But not a spine-tingling faith which brings us out in goose-bumps, just enough belief to engage God's power. We simply need to believe that God can do what is needed, and to be ready to act as his hands and his voice.

Matthew 9:2 ☐
9:22 ☐
9:29 ☐
Mark 6:1–6 ☐

Sometimes God will give us a special gift of faith when he wants to do something remarkable: he does this by adding his faith to ours. More commonly, our simple belief in God is all the faith we need.

4.   Action

When we are ministering, the Spirit guides us along his own creative path. He might prompt us to do something unusual – like Jesus anointing a man's eyes with saliva. But this does not mean that we should ever do the same thing again unless he clearly instructs us.

However, there are ten basic principles which usually make sense.

1. We should show Christ's love, smile, use first names, and relax. God performs the miracle, not us.

2. We should ask the Holy Spirit to provide us with guidance, boldness, power and purity.

3. We should keep our eyes open – some information is received only by watching how the person responds to God's power.

4. We should listen attentively to God and speak whatever he puts into our mind. He may tell us to command a growth to be removed. He may ask us to announce faith, freedom or blessing. He might ask us to squeeze the person's hand and remain silent.

5. We should ask God whether it is right to touch the person or not. If it seems best, we can gently place our hands on the clothing nearest to the affected part of the body.

6. We should ask the person, 'Do you feel anything?' 'What is happening?' We need to ensure that they keep us informed about the progress.

7. We should watch for bodily reactions to the Spirit. The person may shake, stiffen or fall. Their breathing may change. They may tingle, laugh or cry. Their eyes may moisten – and so on.

Although these reactions often indicate that God is at work, they are only the body's reaction to God. A strong physical reaction does not evidence a greater work, nor does the absence of any bodily reaction mean nothing is happening in the spiritual realm.

8. If a bodily reaction does takes place, we should help the person to be as comfortable as possible. But we need to ignore the reaction and press on with the ministry.

9. We should continually encourage the person and help them to feel at ease.

10. We can use the gift of tongues, and should stop ministering when the Spirit's agenda has been achieved, or when we can't think of anything else to say or do, or when the person asks us to stop, or when anyone seems tired.

5.   Humility

Many people are attracted to ministry for wrong reasons. We should seek the holy anonymity of the Spirit and aim to focus attention on God alone, without basking in any associated glory.

No man or woman can work a miracle. The highest we can aim is to be an unprofitable servant whom God tips off a few minutes in advance of a miracle. We are lowly couriers, not the manufacturer.

Obvious and unassumed humility is a key demonstration of the character of the Spirit. Just as we need power *and* purity, so humility must accompany signs and wonders.

DISCIPLESHIP WITH THE SPIRIT

Luke 17:15–19 ☐

John 5:14 ☐

9:35–38 ☐

In Luke 17:15–19, John 5:14 & 9:35–38 we see how Jesus followed through *after* ministry with people he had helped.

People often do not receive everything from God when we minister to them for the first time. We may need to go back to them several times to help them receive whatever God has for them.

When we are mulling over what has happened, the Spirit frequently puts a thought into our minds and we wish that we had said this or done that. It is often right to go back to the person and briefly mention this 'afterthought' – much as Jesus seems to have done in John 5:14.

John 5:14 ☐

After ministry

When, in partnership with the Spirit, we have finished ministering to someone we need to ask our partner what we should do next.

It may be right to say and do nothing except pray. But – if the ministry has been extended and we have sought God for healing, freedom or special direction – it is usually good to encourage the person to offer praise and thanksgiving.

When we have prayed for healing, and the person has been receiving special medical care or using prescribed drugs, we should encourage the person to visit their doctor. This seems to have been Jesus' concern in Matthew 8:4.

Matthew 8:4 ☐

If we are living with the Spirit and eager to develop Jesus' ministry, most of the people we minister to will be *unbelievers*. It is good to explain the Good News to them, and point them towards the next step in Christian commitment, whether repentance, baptism, receiving the Spirit, or joining a local congregation.

It is helpful to sit down a few days after ministering and go through what happened. We can learn much from our mistakes if we are prepared to acknowledge them. There will be moments when we will have been too timid and others when we will have been too forceful. We should reflect honestly on what happened and ask the Spirit to show us where we were out-of-step with him.

Most importantly, we must recognise that we may have a God-given responsibility for the person we have met. Obviously we will pray for their safety and spiritual development, but we will need the Spirit's guidance as to whether we should become more closely involved.

We know that the Spirit has come alongside us to encourage, comfort, teach and direct us. When we are living in him, we will naturally be led alongside people to help and encourage them in a similar way.

Corporate ministry

The principle of partnership runs through the Bible. For example:

- One solitary individual cannot reflect the image of the triune God; it needs a relationship.

- The promises of Matthew 18:19–20 are made to two or three, not to one.

- Matthew 10:1–16 shows how Jesus sent the Twelve to minister in partnership, and Luke 10:1–20 describes how seventy-two others were sent in the same way.

- Protection from the enemy forces is granted to the church, not to isolated individuals.

This does not mean that we refuse to minister if nobody else is with us. The book of Acts contains many examples of believers who were sent by the Spirit to minister on their own – for example, Philip in Acts 8:26–40 and Ananias in Acts 9:10–19. But Philip was one of the Seven, the apostles worked mainly in pairs, and Paul always ministered with close companions.

When we are ministering in a partnership, it is easier to lead the people we have helped into similar relationships. Our ministry must build the people we help into a corporate life which reflects the relationship of the Triune God.

Acts 2:41 does not record that three thousand were converted, it states that they were 'added to them'. Their salvation had an essential corporate dynamic.

The signs and wonders ministry described in Acts 2:43 is surrounded by a description of community life. On through Acts, it is not possible to imagine ministry apart from the Christian community. When the Holy Spirit led New Testament believers to needy people, they brought them into the church.

So, when we have ministered to people today, we must encourage them to become part of a living, loving local congregation.

Although we have focused on the Spirit's work in individual believers, we must realise that the Spirit wants to knit us together in dynamic communities which are full of the presence of God.

Matthew
18:19–20 ☐

Matthew 10:1–16 ☐
Luke 10:1–20 ☐

Acts 8:26–40 ☐
9:10–19 ☐

Acts 2:43 ☐

Community Life

The Spirit is the witness to Jesus. He pours power and purity into our lives so that we become ever more accurate witnesses to the character of Jesus. But he also is working to bring us *together* under Christ.

Ephesians 1:3–23 shows the extent to which we are called together. Ephesians 2 is all about 'us together'. We are 'fellow citizens with the saints and members of the household of God'. We are 'joined together'. We are growing 'into a holy temple in the Lord'. We are 'being built together for a habitation of God in the Spirit'.

Sometimes it seems easier just to get on with God's work on our own. Yet Jesus submitted to and depended on people in a quite striking way. For example, he meekly submitted to:

- his parents
- John's baptism
- the synagogue authorities
- political leaders
- Jewish priests
- Pilate

If we want to live and minister with his authority, we need to live as he lived – voluntarily under the authority of others.

We have been rescued from sin to be part of a healing community, a loving community, a community which is throbbing with the life of the Holy Spirit, a community which is constantly reaching out to the people round about. We should be doing everything possible to develop such a community and to draw the people we help into the Spirit's common life.

Together in the Spirit, we are equipped to exercise authority over all evil powers in our area.

Together with the Spirit we will be being inspired to discover a life of service which follows Christ's sacrificial, foot-washing example. We share his authority to reach out in his name with healing to the sick and broken-hearted around us.

Together in the Spirit, we are should be living a life which is slowly moving towards Christ's perfection. With his help, we should

Ephesians 1:3–23 ☐

Ephesians 2 ☐

be beginning to understand our neighbours with the insight and sympathy of Christ.

And together, in and with the Spirit, we should be learning to radiate God's love, to shine with his light and truth, to display more and more of his glory.

We have received the Spirit from Christ to make God's presence felt in our streets in deeply practical ways – and we do this as partners with the Spirit, living in the holy presence of God.

A CHALLENGE

By now, you should have been thoroughly introduced to the Spirit.

- You know that he brings God's power – so that you can know Jesus better and make him better known to the needy world around you.

- You know that he brings God's purity to transform you into the image of Jesus – so that the people around you can see Jesus and be drawn to him.

- You know that the Spirit brings the presence of Jesus to you – so that you can reveal Jesus' presence to the world by speaking his words and doing his deeds.

As a believer who knows the Spirit, it is your function to reveal God's glory in and to the world. You have been chosen to show God's holy character to the people around you.

You can do it – but only in and with the Spirit. Through the Spirit, Jesus is urging you into powerful holy action – to heal the broken-hearted, to feed the hungry, to welcome outcasts, to deal with demons, to go about doing the good deeds he directs.

In the Spirit, Jesus is drawing near to you. He wants to transform you into his likeness, and to equip and motivate you to reach out to the world with his love and mercy.

Please do not resist the Spirit – instead, respond to him with loving submission and become his devoted partner.

ACTIVITIES for individuals and small groups

the spirit in the old testament

THE BLOWING OF GOD

Throughout the Old Testament, the Holy Spirit is called 'the Spirit' or 'the Spirit of God'. The English word 'Spirit' is always a translation of the Hebrew word *ruach*. It is vital we understand what this word means.

What do you understand ruach to mean?

....

....

In Ezekiel 37:1–14, ruach is translated in three different ways. What are these, and what do they teach us?

....

....

No English word accurately captures all the meanings of *ruach*. The words 'blow' and 'Spirit' come closest to its meaning.

What are the strengths and weaknesses of 'blow' and 'Spirit' as translations of ruach?

....

....

....

What should we imagine when we read about the Spirit in the Old Testament?

....

....

....

....

....

WORD PICTURES

The Spirit is described in the Old Testament in four more images which help us grasp his character and appreciate his activities more fully.

1.   Water

Please read these verses and list the different ways that the Bible uses water as a symbol of the Spirit and his work: Exodus 29:4; Leviticus 11:40; 15:5–33; Numbers 8:7; Psalm 36:9; 46:4; Isaiah 30:25; 55:1; Jeremiah 2:13; 17:13; Ezekiel 36:25–28; 47:1–12; Joel 3:18; Zechariah 13:1 & 14:8.

....

....

....

....

....

2.   Fire

In the Old Testament, fire was a symbol of God's intervention in history and of the way his Spirit purified human hearts and cleansed them for service.

What do we learn about the Spirit is these passages? Genesis 15:17; Exodus 3:2; 13:21; 19:18; Deuteronomy 4:11–12, 24; 2 Kings 6:17; Psalm 66:12; Isaiah 4:2–6; 6:6–9; 43:2; 66:15; Ezekiel 22:18–22; Daniel 3:25; Zechariah 13:9; Malachi 3:2–3 & 4:1.

....

....

....

....

3.   Oil

In Old Testament days, oil had several practical uses. What were they? And what application do they have in the Spirit?

....

....

....

Anointing with oil symbolised the equipping of a priest or king for service with the necessary resource of God's Spirit.

What do we learn about anointing and the Spirit in 1 Samuel 10:1–9; 16:13; Isaiah 61:1–3 & Zechariah 4:1–14.?

....

....

....

....

....

4.   Dove

What were the practical uses of doves in biblical days?

....

....

....

What do these passages teach about doves? Genesis 8:1–12; Leviticus 5:7–10; Song of Songs 2:14; 5:2 & 6:9.

....

....

....

....

Which prophet was Mr Dove? What meaning does his life and work suggest for the Spirit 'coming like a dove' on Jesus?

....

....

....

....

THE WORK OF THE SPIRIT

The phrase 'the Spirit' or 'the Spirit of God' appears nearly 100 times in the Old Testament. Every time, it describes God at work, God bringing change, God making a difference. The scriptural material seems to show that God's Spirit is involved in seven activities.

What do these passages teach about the Spirit's work in the Old Testament?

1.   Genesis 1:2; 2:7; Psalm 33:6; Job 26:13; 33:4

....

....

2.   Psalm 104:29–30; Isaiah 34:16 & 40:7

....

....

3.   Numbers 11:29; 24:2; 1 Samuel 10; 19:18–24; 2 Samuel 23:2; 2 Chronicles 12:18; 15:1; Nehemiah 9:30; Job 32:8; Isaiah 61:1–4; Ezekiel 2:2; 11:24; 37:1–2; Micah 3:8; Joel 2:28; Zechariah 7:12

....

....

....

....

4.   Nehemiah 9:20; Psalms 143:10; Isaiah 48:16 & 63:10–14

....

....

5.   Psalm 51 10–12; Isaiah 44:3–5; Ezekiel 11:19–20; 36:25–27; 39:29; Joel 2:28–32

....

....

....

6.   Genesis 41:33–42; Numbers 11:16–29; Judges 3:10; 6:34; 11:29; 13:25; 14:19, 15;
          1 Samuel 10:10; 11:6; 16:13 & 19:20–23; 2 Kings 2:9–15; Isaiah 11:1–5 & 42:1–4

....

....

....

....

7.   Exodus 31:1–3; 35:30–35; 1 Kings 7:14; Haggai 2:4–9 & Zechariah 4:6–10

....

....

THE HOLY SPIRIT

The Spirit is called 'the Holy Spirit' only twice in the Old Testament. Why are these passages so important?

....

....

What does Psalm 51:7–15 suggest is associated with the Holy Spirit?

....

....

....

....

What does Isaiah 63:7–14 suggest is associated with the Holy Spirit?

....

....

....

....

the spirit in the new testament

THE BLOWING GOD

Pneuma, the Greek word which is translated as 'Spirit', is another picture word which carries the meaning of a powerful wind as well as a personal spirit. *Pneuma* is used widely in the New Testament.

What is pneuma *used to show in these passages?*

Matthew 4:1; 5:3; 8:16; Luke 1:17; 4:18; 8:55; John 3:8; 6:63; Acts 7:59; 17:16; Romans 1:4; 7:6; 7:22; 8:15; 8:25; 1 Corinthians 4:21; 14:12; 15:45; 16:18; 2 Corinthians 4:13, 16; 12:18; Ephesians 4:23; 1 Timothy 3:16; 2 Timothy 1:7; Philemon 25; Hebrews 1:14; 12:23; 1 Peter 3:4; 3:19; Revelation 1:10; 4:2; 11:11.

....

....

....

....

....

....

We must bear the richness of *pneuma* in mind when we read about the Spirit. It is too easy to have a limited view of the Spirit – we must appreciate the big biblical picture of his work.

NAMES AND TITLES

The Spirit is given many different names and titles in the New Testament.

List as many as you can.

....

....

....

....

....

....

Check your answer with these verses: Matthew 1:18; 4:1; 10:20; 12:32; 22:43; 28:19; John 14:17; Acts 5:9; 8:39; 16:7; Romans 8:2; 8:9; 8:11; 8:15; 1 Corinthians 2:11; 6:11; 2 Corinthians 3:3; 3:18; Galatians 4:6; Ephesians 1:13; 4:30; Philippians 1:19; Hebrews 9:14; 10:29; 1 Peter 4:14.

THE PERSONAL NATURE OF THE SPIRIT

The New Testament uses many different ways to show that the Spirit of the Old Testament is a distinct, divine person.

How does Jesus emphasise the personhood of the Spirit in John 14:26; 15:26; 16:8, 13, 14?

....

....

....

Jesus and the apostles clearly recognised that the person of the Spirit was active in the Old Testament, and that references to God's breath meant the Spirit's personal activity.

How do these passages link together to reveal the truth of the Spirit's personhood?

Mark 12:36, Acts 1:16; 4:25 and 2 Samuel 23:2

....

Luke 4:18–21 and Isaiah 61:1–4

....

John 3:5–10 and Ezekiel 36:25–27 & 37:1–14

....

Acts 2:16–18 and Joel 2:28–29

....

What personal activities of the Spirit can we read about in these verses?

John 14:26; 15:26; 16:7–15; Acts 2:4; 5:3–4; 8:29; 13:2; 16:6–7; Romans 8:14–27; Galatians 4:6; 5:17–18; Ephesians 4:30

....

....

....

How do these verses show that the Spirit is divine?

Matthew 28:19; Acts 5:3–4; 1 Corinthians 12:4–6; 2 Corinthians 13:14; Ephesians 1:3–14; 2:18; 3:14–19; 4:4–6; 2 Thessalonians 2:13–14; 1 Peter 1:2; & Revelation 1:4–5

....

....

JOHN'S ANNOUNCEMENT

Why is John the Baptist's announcement that Jesus 'will baptise you with Holy Spirit and fire' so important?

....

....

Which Old Testament pictures of the Spirit would John's listeners have remembered?

....

Which Old Testament passages about the Spirit was John pointing to?

....

How are these passages relevant? Isaiah 1:25; 4:3–6; Daniel 7:10; Zechariah 13:9; Malachi 3:2–3

....

....

LUKE'S SPECIAL PHRASE

Who does Luke describe as being 'filled with the Spirit'?

Luke 1:15, 41, 67; 4:1; Acts 2:4; 4:8; 6:5; 7:55; 9:17; 11:23 & 13:52

....

....

How do Matthew 27:48 and John 19:29 help us understand the idea of 'being filled'?

....

....

Luke uses the same phrase to describe *both* the experience of becoming filled *and* the result of being filled – Luke 1:41 & 4:1; Acts 2:4 & 4:8.

Have you been filled with the Spirit? Are you filled with the Spirit?

....

JESUS' MINISTRY

Why did Jesus need to be filled with the Spirit before he began his ministry?

....

....

What is the difference between Jesus in Luke 4:1 and 4:14? How did this come about?

....

....

Luke 4:16–27 describes Jesus quoting from Isaiah 61 and applying it to himself. Acts 10:38 reflects on this and states that – once and for all – God became 'with him'. Because of his anointing, Jesus could do that which – as a man – he had previously been unable to do.

How did the Spirit help Jesus in these passages?

Matthew 12:28; Luke 10:21; Acts 1:2; Hebrews 9:14

....

....

THE PARAKLETOS

The New Testament records that Jesus taught little about the Spirit until the Last Supper – John 13–17. At that farewell meal, Jesus explained it was to the apostles' advantage that he left. In John 16:7, Jesus said that the *Parakletos* would not come unless he departed.

What does 'Parakletos' mean?

....

In what way is the Parakletos *like Jesus?*

....

What do we learn about the Spirit's work in these verses?

John 14:25–27; 15:26; 16:7–11; 16:13;

....

....

What is the essence of the Spirit's work?

....

....

How is this work evidenced in your life?

....

....

....

PENTECOST

What did the feast of Pentecost celebrate in New Testament days?

....

....

Why did God choose Pentecost to empower the Church?

....

....

Acts 2:1–41 tells the story of Pentecost.

What was the baptistery? ....

Who were the candidates? ....

Who was the baptiser? ....

Who was the element? ....

What was the result? ....

What was the significance of the fire?

....

....

What was the significance of the wind?

....

....

What differences did Pentecost make?

....

....

What did Pentecost prove?

....

....

THE AGE OF THE SPIRIT

Since Pentecost, we have been living in 'the Age of the Spirit'. This is different from the period before Pentecost. The main differences is the total availability of the Holy Spirit. Until Pentecost, the Spirit was given to only a few believers. But – at Pentecost – there was no limitation on the giving of the Spirit by God, and no restriction on the receiving of the Spirit by men and women. Since then, every believer has been able to receive the Holy Spirit.

The 'Age of the Spirit' is characterised by:

1.   Continuous witness

The Spirit continuously witnesses to Jesus, gives glory to Jesus, and focuses the world's attention on the only Son of God.

How does the Spirit witness to Jesus?

....

....

How, practically, do you co-operate with the Spirit in his witnessing?

....

....

....

2.   Holy lifestyle

Instead of drawing attention to himself, the Spirit always points people to the Son and to the Father. This humility is a key characteristic of the people who are controlled by the Spirit.

What is the lifestyle of those who are led by the Spirit in his Age?

....

....

3.   Basic truth

John 14:26 & 16:13 show that the *Parakletos* will be a teacher. Since Pentecost, the Spirit has been the church's teacher – gently guiding us towards the truth.

What and how does the Spirit teach us?

....

....

What, practically, has the Spirit taught you most recently?

....

....

4.   Constant change

The Spirit is the wind – the blowing – of God which we can neither predict nor control. We must recognise this means that he will often introduce surprising new developments.

What major changes did the Spirit bring in Acts?

....

....

What major changes has the Spirit most recently brought to you?

....

....

5.   Christ's presence

John 14:21–23 is pivotal to our understanding of the Spirit. It is his work to make the presence of Christ a real experience for all who show that they love Jesus by obeying his words.

How, in principle, does the Spirit reveal Jesus to us?

....

....

How, practically, has the Spirit revealed Jesus to you?

....

....

the spirit and jesus

By introducing the Spirit in John 14:15–18 as *allos parakletos*, Jesus made it plain that the Spirit would be 'another the same' as himself. If we want to know what the Spirit is like, we have only to look at the biblical records about Jesus.

But although Jesus is fully God, he is also the Ideal Human – when we look at Jesus, we also see what we are meant to be like. This means Jesus' life and ministry reveals the Spirit's nature and also the relationship that we are meant to have with the Spirit.

THE ANOINTED

What are the Hebrew and Greek words for 'The Anointed?

....

What do these verse show the purpose of Jesus' anointing to be?

Luke 4:18–21; Mark 8:29; Acts 10:38

....

What do these verses teach about Jesus' anointing?

Matthew 3:13–17; 4:1; Mark 1:9–12, Luke 3:21–22; 4:1–27; John 1:32–34; 3:34; Acts 10:38

....

....

JESUS' MODEL MINISTRY

Jesus' ministry had four themes which are emphasised in each of the four Gospels.

1.   *Jesus was a mighty king who was concerned to found a kingdom.* He ruled over nature and disease. He conquered demons, healed lepers were and revived the dead. When we share Jesus' anointing, something of his kingly authority should be seen in us.

What is your experience of this side of Jesus' ministry in the Spirit?

....

....

....

....

2. *Jesus was a suffering servant who came to serve and offer himself as a sacrifice.* He came to save lost people who were powerless to save themselves, to make atonement for every sin, to be a substitute for all people, and to bear God's wrath against sin. When we share Jesus' anointing, we will willingly embrace service, sacrifice and suffering.

What is your experience of this side of Jesus' ministry in the Spirit?

....

....

....

....

3. *Jesus came as the ideal human being to show us how to live and die.* Jesus was tested in every possible way. He was subject to ordinary conflict and emotions, yet remained without sin. He was the sympathetic friend of sinners. He was the perfect example of forgiveness. When we are filled with the same Spirit, we will live with his holiness.

What is your experience of this side of Jesus' ministry in the Spirit?

....

....

....

....

4. *Jesus came as the revelation of God to reproduce the divine nature in us.* Everything he said and did, revealed God. He emphasised his oneness with the Father. He explained that his words and deeds were the Father's. Through Christ, we know what the Father is like. In a similar way, our Spirit-filled lives and ministries should also point people to the Father.

Jesus offers us exactly the same anointing as he had, calls us to carry out the same work he did. His ministry is the perfect model for us today. However we must apply four basic principles which undergirded Jesus' model ministry.

1. Jesus ministered with prayer

Prayer was a secret of Jesus' dynamic ministry. If we want to follow him, intercessory prayer will dominate our ministries too.

When, where and why do these verses show Jesus praying?

Mark 1:35, 6:46, 14:32; Luke 3:21; 5:16; 6:12; 9:18; 9:28–29; 22:41; 23:34; 24:30; John 17.

....

....

....

....

....

....

2. He ministered with obedience

What is the principle behind the words and deeds of Jesus which is recorded in John 5:19, 30; 6:38; 7:28–29; 8:26, 28–29; 10:18 & 12:49–50?

....

....

....

3. Jesus ministered with compassion

Jesus ministered not to attract attention to himself, but because he loved needy people and cared about their needs. Mark 1:41; 6:34 & 10:21 describe Christ's compassion.

To what extent do you allow compassion to direct and motivate your actions?

....

....

4.   Jesus ministered with the Spirit's help

Jesus had tremendous skill in ministering according to the gifts of the Spirit. In fact we see all the New Testament gifts in Jesus' ministry except tongues and interpretation.

Which spiritual gift is Jesus using in each of these passages?

Matthew 4:23–25 ....

Matthew 16:17–23 ....

Mark 5:21–43 ....

Mark 6:30–52 ....

Mark 11:20–25 ....

Luke 13:10–17 ....

John 1:47–50 ....

John 2:1–11 ....

John 2:19 ....

John 4:16–20 ....

John 11:41–42 ....

Jesus did not depend on a pattern or formula when he was ministering – he depended on the help and prompting of the Spirit. He ministered differently on almost every occasion.

What habits or patterns are there in your ministry? How predictable are your words and actions when you are ministering to someone? How should this change?

....

....

....

JESUS' MINISTRY TODAY

Jesus' ministry did not end at the cross. Matthew 28:18–20; Mark 16:15–18 and Luke 24:44–49 describe Jesus' charge to his disciples to continue his ministry on earth – and his promise to carry on working with them.

How was Jesus working in these verses? Acts 3:6; 5:12–16; 8:4–8; 9:32–43 & 16:6–10

....

....

....

....

....

....

Jesus has ministered like this through the centuries. It is now our responsibility to continue the same work. We do not have to do this on our own, in our own strength and ability.

What are the four vital things that Jesus does today to help us minister?

Romans 8:34 & Hebrews 7:25 ....

Ephesians 4:11–12 ....

Matthew 28:20 & Mark 16:20 ....

Ephesians 2:15–16 & John 17:20–26 ....

What do these passages teach about the character and function of the church?

1 Corinthians 1:2 ....

....

1 Corinthians 3:16 ....

....

2 Corinthians 11:2 ....

....

Ephesians 1:23 ....

....

1 Peter 2:9 ....

....

receiving the spirit

John's announcement is the only summary of the purpose of Jesus' ministry which appears in all four Gospels. John's use of the phrase *Holy Spirit* points directly to Psalm 51 & Isaiah 63.

What does Psalm 51:1–17 suggest that having the Holy Spirit relates to?

....

....

....

....

What does Isaiah 63:7–14 suggest that having the Holy Spirit relates to?

....

....

....

....

What do Old Testament ideas about the Spirit suggest being baptised in the Spirit will mean?

....

....

....

....

Why does John link the Holy Spirit with fire? What does this imply?

....

....

....

The New Testament contains five phrases which all describe an encounter with the Holy Spirit. Each phrases sheds some light on a different aspect of this experience.

BAPTISED IN THE HOLY SPIRIT

This phrase occurs seven times in most English versions of the New Testament – Matthew 3:11; Mark 1:8; Luke 3:16; John 1:33; Acts 1:5; 11:16; 1 Corinthians 12:13.

What is the significance of the word 'baptism'?

....

....

What is the significance of the baptism occurring at Pentecost?

....

....

FILLED WITH THE HOLY SPIRIT

This expression is used twelve times in the New Testament to describe the way that people receive the Spirit – Luke 1:15; 1:41; 1:67; 4:1; Acts 2:4; 4:8; 6:5; 7:55; 9:17; 11:23; 13:52 & Ephesians 5:18.

Why is it important that the phrase describes what happened before, at and after Pentecost?

....

....

Why is it important that the same phrase is used to describe the process of becoming filled as well as the ongoing state of being filled?

....

....

....

How does the sponge picture help us to understand 'becoming filled' and 'being filled?

....

....

ANOINTED WITH THE SPIRIT

Who was anointed in the Old Testament? What does this suggest about our anointing?

....

....

What is the purpose of our anointing?

....

....

How often should we be anointed?

....

....

SEALED WITH THE SPIRIT

What is a legal seal? What does it show? What does this teach us about receiving the Spirit?

....

....

What do 2 Corinthians 1:22 & Ephesians 1:13 & 4:30 teach about our sealing?

....

....

RECEIVING THE SPIRIT

How do Acts 8:14–17 & 19:2–7 show that receiving the Spirit is separate from conversion?

....

....

A DISTINCT EXPERIENCE

Conversion is a process which includes repentance, faith, forgiveness of sins, baptism in water and receiving the Spirit.

What do John 3:1–8; Romans 8:1–14 & 1 Corinthians 2:10–14 teach about the Spirit's work?

....

....

....

It is possible to be a believer and not to be baptised in the Spirit. This is accomplished by Jesus. He is the baptiser; the Holy Spirit is the element.

List as many scriptural examples as you can of believers who had been accepted by God but who had not been baptised in the Spirit.

....

....

....

What is your experience of receiving the Spirit?

....

....

....

....

....

What difference has the Spirit made to your life and ministry?

....

....

....

....

the power of the spirit

The most common Greek word for power is *dunamis*: this describes a moral, physical or spiritual ability which resides in a person or object. It is the explosive energy which makes things happen! *Dunamis* is the supernatural power of God by which miracles occur, preaching is made effective, and people are strengthened to endure terrible persecutions and adversity.

The New Testament shows that the Spirit's dunamis *power has a wide variety of applications. What do these verses show God's power to be for?*

Acts 1:8 ....

Acts 4:33 ....

Acts 6:8 ....

Acts 10:38 ....

Romans 15:13 ....

Romans 15:18–19 ....

1 Corinthians 2:4–5 ....

2 Corinthians 6:6–10 ....

2 Corinthians 12:9 ....

Ephesians 3:16 ....

Ephesians 6:10 ....

Philippians 4:13 ....

Colossians 1:11 ....

1 Thessalonians 1:5 ....

2 Timothy 1:7 ....

POWER FOR PUBLIC PROCLAMATION

In the Old Testament, the anointing with the Spirit gave the prophets the power to receive, understand and speak God's thoughts. By the Spirit, they knew what God wanted them to say and they had his authority and *dunamis* to say it aloud in public. In the New Testament, the Spirit enabled *all* believers who were filled with him both to know what to say and to speak it with a power and authority that they did not naturally possess.

What difference has the Spirit made to your public speaking or witnessing about Jesus?

....

....

....

....

....

....

....

....

....

....

POWER FOR MIRACLES

Acts 6:8 shows that power was the key to Stephen's miracles, and Romans 15:18–19 underlines that it is the power of God's Spirit. The Spirit gives power for miracles essentially in the context of proclaiming the good news about Jesus to those who do not yet believe.

In each of these passages from Acts about miracles:

1. *Is the context teaching, worship, pastoral care or evangelism?*

2. *Is the consequence conversions, persecution, challenge or nothing?*

3. *Is the person helped a follower or an unbeliever?*

Passage	Context	Consequence	Person
2:43			
3:1–10			
5:12–16			
6:8			
8:4–8			

Passage	Context	Consequence	Person
9:8–19			
9:32–35			
9:36–43			
14:3			
14: 8–10			
14:19–20			
16:16–18			
19:11–12			
20:7–12			
28:7–10			

POWER FOR WARFARE

Ephesians 6:10–20 & 1 Peter 5:8 show that all Christians are involved in a struggle with the enemy. 2 Corinthians 10:4–6 promises that the Spirit gives us all the power we need for this sort of spiritual warfare.

The Spirit gives us the power to confront demons, to resist the devil, and to say 'no' to cravings for whatever 'the world, the flesh and the devil' seem to be offering. He gives us the strength to be patient with people, to keep our tempers, to stand firm under pressure, to love the unlovable – in fact, to do all the godly things that the enemy tries to ensure we do not do.

2 Corinthians 12:9–10 helps us to put our own problems into perspective and to think about them biblically.

How has the Spirit helped you in your struggle with the enemy?

....

....

....

....

....

POWER FOR HOPE AND PERSEVERANCE

Most Christians know some of God's promises. But we need the Spirit's power to translate these promises into an experience which fills us with hope in the face of bad news. We need to pray Paul's Romans 15:13 intercession for each other.

2 Corinthians 6:3–10 & Colossians 1:11 help us appreciate Paul's attitude to difficult circumstances. He knew that God gives patience and grace to endure troubles. We must remember that God's gift of *dunamis* for endurance helps us to overcome hardships.

How has the Spirit helped you to persevere and endure?

....

....

....

....

POWER FOR WITNESS TO JESUS

Every aspect of the Spirit's power is given to enable us to know Jesus better, and to help us reveal Jesus more clearly to the needy world around us. The real test of true spiritual power is whether or not it brings people into a deep knowledge and understanding of Jesus.

Why do you want to receive the Spirit's power?

....

....

How do you control and use the Spirit's power?

....

....

How should you speak about God's power in an evangelistic setting?

....

....

....

....

the purity of the spirit

Although we often talk about 'the Spirit', we know that he is 'the *Holy* Spirit'. His name reveals his nature. He is perfectly holy.

What does 'holy' mean?

....

In what way is the Father, the Son and the Spirit holy?

....

Holiness is not something we aspire to or attain; rather it is the state into which God, in his grace, has called us and in which we live. Purity (like power) is a practical consequence of that state – it is a manifestation of the Spirit which is seen in our conduct.

PURITY FROM SIN

Sin is rebellion against God and any form of self-will in thought or word or deed.

What do these verses teach about sin?

Proverbs 6:16–19 ....

Isaiah 4:4 ....

Isaiah 61:8 ....

Jeremiah 44:4 ....

Ezekiel 36:25–27 ....

Zechariah 13:1 ....

Malachi 3:2 ....

John 13:10 ....

John 15:3 ....

Acts 22:16 ....

Romans 3:9 ....

Romans 7:20–23 ....

1 Corinthians 6:11 ....

2 Corinthians 7:1 ....

Ephesians 5:3–5 ....

Ephesians 5:25–27 ....

2 Timothy 2:20–22 ....

Hebrews 9:11–14 ....

Hebrews 10:22 ....

1 John 1:7–9 ....

1 John 3:3 ....

The Spirit is God's agent of purity. He makes us 'born again'. He provides us with the 'new heart' which creates the possibility – which did not previously exist – of living in purity and of obeying God's commandments. He shapes our lives and regenerates us. He enables us to receive the very nature of Christ – and to become more like him throughout our earthly lives.

THE BELIEVER'S INNER STRUGGLE

There are two opposed sets of desires in every Christian: those which express the 'natural self-willing and rebelling against God' nature of fallen humanity, and those which express the 'supernatural God-honouring and God loving' nature implanted in us by the Spirit.

Galatians 5:16 recognises the reality of our struggle, shows that walking or living in the Spirit is the way forward, and insists that we can resist the fallen desires which assault us.

What do these verses teach about the struggle?

Romans 6:17–7:6 ....

Romans 7:6 ....

Romans 8:4 ....

Romans 8:13 ....

Galatians 5:13–14 ....

Galatians 5:16–25 ....

1 Thessalonians 4:1–8 ....

What has the Spirit helped you to discover about yourself?

....

....

PURITY THROUGH STRENGTH TO CHANGE

The Spirit of truth makes as aware of our faults and failings, and draws our attention to the ways we disappoint God. He highlights our bad habits and urges us to take note of passages like 2 Corinthians 7:1 and to cleanse ourselves from the filthiness of the flesh and the spirit.

Please read these passages: Romans 6:17–7:6; 8:13–14; Galatians 5:13; 1 Thessalonians 4:1–8.

What is God's responsibility for your purity?

....

....

What is your responsibility for your purity?

....

....

....

What does the enemy seek to do about this?

....

....

....

PURITY THROUGH TRANSFORMATION

The spiritual struggle is not self-effort. We *are* washed, *are* cleansed and *are* sanctified. God, by the Spirit, works in our lives to bring purity, to shape us in his image. 2 Corinthians 3:18 shows that 'we all *are being transformed* into the same image ... by the Spirit'. Few passages describe this better than Galatians 5:16–26. It contains a word-picture of the truly Christ-like character which supernatural develops in those who stay living in and with the Spirit.

To what extent has the fruit of the Spirit developed in your life? What aspects of the fruit are least developed in you?

....

....

....

....

PURITY FOR WITNESS

The Spirit's main work is bringing glory to Jesus, focusing the world's attention on him, drawing sinful people into the love and grace of God. This means that the main reason for his purity is to show people the true nature of Jesus.

We are called to be pure and are given purity so that people around us will see Jesus. Purity, like power, is essentially for witness.

Why are you asking to be pure?

....

....

....

Why does God want you to be pure?

....

....

....

What areas of your life need to be transformed?

....

....

....

performance and the spirit

We know that we cannot make ourselves powerful or pure. If we want to glorify God and share his goodness, we will sow our lives in the most favourable place – in the Spirit.

The same principle applies in every area of the Spirit. The gifts are not an ability to do something, but his work through us. They are his energy, not our activity.

What gifts have you received from the Spirit? When did you receive them? How do you use them?

....
....
....
....

Gifts follows the same principle as power and purity. They are an expression of the Spirit's nature, and we know them when we are in the Spirit. Isaiah 11:2 lists seven attributes of the Spirit which have their application in 11:3–5 and their consequence in 11:6–10.

What do these attributes accomplish?

....
....
....
....

How do they relate to the 1 Corinthians 12–14 'gifts'?

....
....

If we have been anointed with the Spirit and are living in the Spirit, we should expect these attributes to be manifested in, around and through us.

THE PERFORMANCE OF SPIRITUAL GIFTS

1 Corinthians 12:1–10 is the most well-known passage about gifts.

What does this passage teach about gifts?

....

....

....

....

....

....

1 Corinthians 12:8–10 identifies nine *gifts*. These are not something exterior to the Spirit. They are manifestations of him – facets of his character – part of his nature.

What is your experience of each of these gifts?

the word of wisdom ....

....

the word of knowledge ....

....

healings ....

....

faith ....

....

miracles ....

....

prophecy ....

....

discernment ....

....

different kinds of tongues ....

....

interpretation or explanation of tongues ....

....

What is the purpose of the gifts?

....

....

....

What do they prove about the people manifesting them?

....

....

....

THE PERFORMANCE OF BODY MINISTRIES

What is the important truth in Ephesians 4:11–12 about ministry?

....

....

What is the main function of ministers?

....

....

....

The Spirit has a role for everyone. He wants us all to take part in ministry. But the heart of his ministry is revealing Jesus and making him better known. Spiritual gifts and body ministry are means to a greater end, not objectives to be attained. They are consequences of the Spirit's work, not the main thrust. He does want to use these things to reveal Jesus. But he also wants us to grasp his heart and to share his main objective.

THE PERFORMANCE OF CHRISTIAN ACTIVITIES

In the last twenty years there has been a fantastic multiplying of Christian activities. Churches have been inspired by the Holy Spirit to reach into their communities in a host of caring ways.

Please list the Christian activities with which you are involved.

....
....
....
....
....

Please list all the Christian activities with which your church is involved.

....
....
....
....
....

Why did these activities begin?

....
....

What is their present purpose?

....
....

To what extent is this purpose being achieved?

....
....

How will the enemy try to spoil these activities?

....
....
....

the presence of the spirit

Mediating or bringing the presence of Christ to the church is the essence of the Spirit's work. God's main aim is making known the personal presence of Jesus in the church and believers.

This is foreshadowed in Psalm 139; Jeremiah 23:23–24; Amos 9:2–5; Genesis 39:2; Exodus 3:12; 33:14–16; Deuteronomy 31:6–8; Joshua 1:5, 9 & Isaiah 43:2–5. This is fulfilled in Jesus – who is introduced by Matthew 1:23 as the 'God with us', the *Emmanuel*, of Isaiah 7:11–16.

The Scriptures show that Jesus is 'God with us'. His presence is the presence of God. Yet Jesus disappeared soon after making his Matthew 28:20 promise, and has not been present on earth in the flesh since his ascension.

How is this promise fulfilled? How is Jesus 'God with us' today?

....
....
....
....

THE PRESENCE OF JESUS

What do these passages teach about the indwelling Spirit and Christ? Romans 8:9; 2 Corinthians 3:17–18; Galatians 4:6; Philippians 1:19 & 1 Peter 1:11

....
....
....
....
....

The simplest way we can understand the ministry of the Spirit is in terms of mediating Christ's presence to us – all his works and activities are part of this mediation. He gives us such a deep knowledge of Jesus' presence with us that three things keep on happening.

1.   The personal fellowship of his presence

In John 16:12–14, Jesus explains how the Spirit will take the things of Jesus and makes them known to us. He will guide us into Jesus' ways and teach us Jesus' truths. We do not hear Jesus audibly. Instead, the Spirit speaks to us in five main ways.

What are these ways?

....

....

How has the Spirit taught you through these ways?

....

....

....

....

2.   The personal transformation of his presence

The longer we spend in the Spirit, the more we become like Jesus. The longer we listen to his words, the more they control our thoughts – and so on.

What were the four main themes of Jesus' ministry?

....

....

Which of these is least evident in your ministry – and why?

....

....

....

3.   The personal assurance of his presence

Romans 8:16 promises that the Spirit will help us know that we are children of God, heirs of God, and joint-heirs with Christ. The presence of Jesus in us by the Spirit is all the proof anyone needs that we are loved and accepted by God. The Spirit's presence is the 'seal' which assures us that we have been forgiven, redeemed, reconciled and welcomed into God's family.

How sure are you that you are loved by God? What is your assurance based upon?

....

....

THE PRESENCE OF GOD

All religions believe that God is real, and credit him with power and benevolence. Christianity is different. Added to our belief that God is everywhere, we claim that he is here with us. The New Testament makes much of the Spirit's power and purity, but it makes even more of him mediating the presence, the word and the activity of God.

What do these passages teach about the Spirit and his work?

Luke 3:22 ....

Luke 4:1 ....

Luke 4: 14–18 ....

Luke 10:21 ....

John 1:32–33 ....

John 3:34 ....

John 7:37–39 ....

John 14:16–21 ....

John 15:26 ....

John 16:7 ....

John 20:22 ....

Acts 2:33 ....

Acts 10:38 ....

Acts 16:7 ....

Romans 8:9–11 ....

2 Corinthians 3:7–18 ....

Galatians 4:6 ....

Philippians 1:19 ....

1 Peter 1:11 ....

1 John 2:20, 27 ....

THE PRESENCE FOR GLORY

In the Old Testament, the expression 'the glory of God' is used in two ways. It refers both to the self-revealed character of God, and also to a visible revelation of God's presence. This means that God's glory shows people both where God is *and* what he is like.

These aspects of God's glory were perfectly fulfilled in Christ. He is the complete self-revelation of God's character and the clearest revelation of God's presence. Since Pentecost, however, it has been the church's function to reveal God's glory in and to the world.

How do you reveal God's glory?

....

....

....

HIS PRESENCE FOR WITNESS

John 14–16 introduce the Spirit's work of bringing glory to Jesus. However 'glory' has become such a 'religious' word that we sometimes forget it is mainly about witness.

In what ways do you attract attention to yourself instead of giving glory to God?

....

....

....

....

....

....

The Spirit fills us with his power so that people will believe Jesus is alive. He saturates us with his holiness so that our behaviour does not cause people to stumble. And he brings the presence of Jesus to our lives so that, wherever we are, we reveal the glorious nature of God.

partnership with the spirit

The Bible uses two pictures to describe our relationship with the Spirit. It uses words like 'baptism' and 'filling' to show that we are placed in the Spirit by Jesus and are called to go on living 'in the Spirit'. Secondly, by introducing the Spirit as the *Parakletos*, the Bible shows that the Spirit is called alongside us to be 'with' us.

Neither picture is adequate on its own to describe the richness of our relationship with the Spirit. We must embrace both ideas and communicate both in our speaking and teaching.

Christian people often use 2 Corinthians 13:14 to bless each other. This illustrates that 'fellowship' is the key biblical word about the Spirit. The Greek word for this is *koinonia* – which means 'sharing together in something purposeful'.

In practice, what does your fellowship with the Spirit mean and involve?

....

....

....

....

DEVELOPING THE MINISTRY OF JESUS

God has forged our partnership with the Spirit so that Jesus' ministry can continue. It is our responsibility to develop this so that Jesus' ministry can become more effective. When we live with the Spirit we hear him prompting us to think like Jesus. We feel his quiet prompting to do this, go there, sit quietly, be silent, send a gift, speak a sentence, and so on.

How do you recognise the Spirit's prompting?

....

....

....

....

....

DEPENDING ON THE SPIRIT

There is tremendous pressure in modern society to appear competent and successful. Yet we only make spiritual progress when we grasp that we cannot do anything on our own. It is only by depending fully on the Spirit that we can begin to minister in the Spirit.

How did Elijah demonstrate his dependence on the Spirit in 1 Kings 18?

....

....

....

How did Jesus demonstrate his dependence on the Spirit in John 5?

....

....

....

How do you demonstrate your dependence on the Spirit?

....

....

....

Depending on the Spirit means relying on our anointing with him by Jesus. This is where developing Christ's ministry and depending on the Spirit draw together.

What is your experience of these aspects of anointing?

the initial anointing ....

....

a continual anointing ....

....

....

special anointing ....

....

....

DISCERNING THE SPIRIT'S AGENDA

Why did Jesus not heal everyone?

....

Who did Jesus heal?

....

We will be disappointed if we take the initiative in ministry or follow our own inclination. We must wait for the Spirit and receive specific directions from him before we proceed.

What are the basic stages of preparing for ministry?

....

....

Which of these stages do you pay least attention to – and why?

....

....

....

DEMONSTRATIONS OF THE SPIRIT

Where were most people ministered to by Jesus?

....

....

What are the implications of this for you?

....

....

....

When the Spirit prompts us to speak and act, there are five simple principles to remember.

1.   Prayer

What do these passages teach about prayer and ministry?

.John 14:12–14 ....

John 16:24 ....

Acts 3:16 ....

Acts 9:17 ....

Acts 9:34 ....

Acts 14:10 ....

Romans 8:26–27 ....

James 5:15 ....

2.   Gifts

Jesus used all the gifts of the Spirit in ministry, except tongues and interpretation, and we can expect to do the same. In ministry, we need to rely on our partner the Spirit to provide what we need, then we should trust the thoughts he gives and act on them.

What gifts have you used in ministry, and how have they helped?

....

....

....

3.   Faith

Some believers think that they need huge amounts of faith for ministry, whereas Jesus suggested that we need only a tiny amount. Matthew 9:2, 22, 29 & Mark 6:1–6 show that we need just enough belief to engage God's power. We simply need to believe that God can do what is needed, and to be ready to act as his hands and his voice.

4.   Action

When we are ministering, the Spirit guides along his own creative path. He might prompt us to do something unusual – like Jesus anointing a man's eyes with saliva. But this does not mean that we should ever do the same thing again unless he clearly instructs us.

Please suggest ten basic, common-sense principles of ministry in the Spirit.

1. ....

2. ....

3. ....

4. ....

5. ....

6. ....

7. ....

8. ....

9. ....

10. ....

5.   Humility

Obvious and unassumed humility is a key demonstration of the character of the Spirit. Just as we need power *and* purity, so humility must accompany signs and wonders.

What would be some wrong reasons for being attracted to ministry?

....

....

What is your reason for being attracted to ministry?

....

....

What are the most important changes the Spirit has asked you to make through these studies?

....

....

....

....

....

....